Option B

Option B

Facing Adversity,
Building Resilience,
and Finding Joy

SHERYL SANDBERG
ADAM GRANT

3 5 7 9 10 8 6 4 2

WH Allen, an imprint of Ebury Publishing,
20 Vauxhall Bridge Road,
London SW1V 2SA

WH Allen is part of the Penguin Random House group of companies
whose addresses can be found at global.penguinrandomhouse.com

 Penguin
Random House
UK

First published in the United Kingdom by WH Allen in 2017
First published in the United States by Alfred A. Knopf in 2017

www.penguin.co.uk

A CIP catalogue record for this book is available from the British Library

HB ISBN 9780753548271
TPB ISBN 9780753548288

Acknowledgement is made to Grey Dog Music (ASCAP) for permission to
reprint excerpted lyrics of "For Good" from the Broadway musical Wicked,
music and lyrics by Stephen Schwartz. Copyright © 2003 by Stephen Schwartz.
All rights reserved. Reprinted by permission of Grey Dog Music (ASCAP).

Book design by Cassandra Pappas
Jacket design by Keith Hayes and the team at MiresBall

Printed and bound in Great Britain by Clays Ltd, St Ives PLC

Penguin Random House is committed to a sustainable future for
our business, our readers and our planet. This book is made from
Forest Stewardship Council® certified paper.

In loving memory of David Bruce Goldberg

October 2, 1967–May 1, 2015

I will always love you, Dave

Contents

Option B

Introduction

THE LAST THING I ever said to him was, "I'm falling asleep."

I met Dave Goldberg in the summer of 1996 when I moved to Los Angeles and a mutual friend invited us both to dinner and a movie. When the film began, I promptly fell asleep, resting my head on Dave's shoulder. Dave liked to tell people that he thought that meant I was into him, until he later learned that—as he put it—"Sheryl would fall asleep anywhere and on anyone."

Dave became my best friend and L.A. began to feel like home. He introduced me to fun people, showed me back streets to avoid traffic, and made sure I had plans on weekends and holidays. He helped me become a bit cooler by introducing me to the internet and playing music I'd never heard. When I broke up with my boyfriend, Dave stepped in to comfort me even though my ex was a former Navy SEAL who slept with a loaded gun under his bed.

Dave used to say that when he met me it was love at first sight, but he had to wait a long time for me to become "smart enough to ditch those losers" and date him. Dave was always a few steps ahead of me. But I caught up eventually. Six and a half years after that movie, we nervously planned a weeklong trip together, knowing it would either take our relationship in a new direction or ruin a great friendship. We married a year later.

Dave was my rock. When I got upset, he stayed calm. When I was worried, he said that everything would be okay. When I wasn't sure what to do, he helped me figure it out. Like all married couples, we had our ups and downs. Still, Dave gave me the experience of being deeply understood, truly supported, and completely and utterly loved. I thought I'd spend the rest of my life resting my head on his shoulder.

Eleven years after our wedding, we went to Mexico to celebrate our friend Phil Deutch's fiftieth birthday. My parents were babysitting our son and daughter in California, and Dave and I were excited to have an adults-only weekend. Friday afternoon, we were hanging out by the pool playing Settlers of Catan on our iPads. For a refreshing change, I was actually winning, but my eyes kept drifting closed. Once I realized that fatigue was going to prevent me from securing Catan victory, I admitted, "I'm falling asleep." I gave in and curled up. At 3:41 p.m., someone snapped a picture of Dave holding his iPad, sitting next to his brother Rob and Phil. I'm asleep on a cushion on the floor in front of them. Dave is smiling.

When I woke up more than an hour later, Dave was no longer in that chair. I joined our friends for a swim, assuming he'd gone to the gym as he'd planned. When I went back to our room to shower and he wasn't there, I was surprised but not concerned. I got dressed for dinner, checked my email, and called our children. Our son was upset because he and his friend had ignored playground rules, climbed a fence, and ripped their sneakers. Through tears, he came clean. I told him that I appreciated his honesty and that Daddy and I would discuss how much he would have to chip in from his allowance for a new pair. Not wanting to live with the uncertainty, our fourth grader pushed me to decide. I told him that this was the kind of decision that Daddy and I made together so I'd have to get back to him the next day.

I left the room and went downstairs. Dave wasn't there. I walked out to the beach and joined the rest of our group. When he wasn't there either, I felt a wave of panic. Something was wrong. I shouted to Rob and his wife Leslye, "Dave isn't here!" Leslye paused, then yelled back, "Where's the gym?" I pointed toward some nearby steps and we started running. I can still feel my breath and body constricting from those words. No one will ever say "Where's the gym?" to me again without causing my heart to race.

We found Dave on the floor, lying by the elliptical machine, his face slightly blue and turned to the left, a small pool of blood under his head. We all screamed. I started CPR. Rob took over from me. A doctor came and took over from him.

The ride in the ambulance was the longest thirty minutes of my life. Dave on a stretcher in the back. The doctor working over him. Me in the front seat where they made me sit, crying and pleading with the doctor to tell me that Dave was still alive. I could not believe how far the hospital was and how few cars moved out of our way. We finally arrived and they carried him behind a heavy wood door, refusing to let me through. I sat on the floor with Marne Levine, Phil's wife and one of my closest friends, holding me.

After what felt like forever, I was led into a small room. The doctor came in and sat behind his desk. I knew what that meant. When the doctor left, a friend of Phil's came over, kissed me on the cheek, and said, "I'm sorry for your loss." The words and the obligatory kiss felt like a flash-forward. I knew I was experiencing something that would happen over and over and over.

Someone asked if I wanted to see Dave to say good-bye. I did—and I did not want to leave. I thought that if I just stayed in that room and held him, if I refused to let go, I would wake up from this nightmare. When his brother Rob, in shock himself, said we had to go, I took a few steps out of the room, then turned around and ran back in, hugging Dave as hard as I could. Eventually, Rob lovingly pulled me off Dave's body. Marne walked me down the long white hall, her arms around my waist holding me up and preventing me from running back into that room.

And so began the rest of my life. It was—and still is—a life I never would have chosen, a life I was completely unprepared for. The unimaginable. Sitting down with my son and daughter and telling them that their father had died. Hearing their screams joined by my own. The funeral. Speeches where people spoke of Dave in the past tense. My house filling up with familiar faces coming up to me again and again, delivering the perfunctory kiss on the cheek followed by those same words: "I'm sorry for your loss."

When we arrived at the cemetery, my children got out of the car and fell to the ground, unable to take another step. I lay on the grass, holding them as they wailed. Their cousins came and lay down with us, all piled up in a big sobbing heap with adult arms trying in vain to protect them from their sorrow.

Poetry, philosophy, and physics all teach us that we don't experience time in equal increments. Time slowed way, way down. Day after day my kids' cries and screams filled the air. In the moments when they weren't crying, I watched them anxiously, waiting for the next instance they might need comfort. My own cries and screams—mostly inside my head but some out loud—filled the rest of the available space. I was in "the void": a vast emptiness that fills your heart and lungs and restricts your ability to think or even breathe.

Grief is a demanding companion. In those early days and weeks and months, it was always there, not just below the surface but on the surface. Simmering, lingering, festering. Then, like a wave, it would rise up and pulse through me, as if it were going to tear my heart right out of my body. In those moments, I felt like I couldn't bear the pain for one more minute, much less one more hour.

I saw Dave lying on the gym floor. I saw his face in the sky. At night, I called out to him, crying into the void: "Dave, I miss you. Why did you leave me? Please come back. I love you . . ." I cried myself to sleep each night. I woke up each morning and went through the motions of my day, often in disbelief that the world continued to turn without him. How could everyone go on as if nothing was different? *Didn't they know?*

Ordinary events became land mines. At Parents' Night, my daughter showed me what she had written eight months before on the first day of school: "I am a second grader. I wonder what will happen in the future." It hit me like a wrecking ball that when she wrote those words, neither she nor I would ever have thought that she would lose her father before she finished second grade. *Second grade.* I looked down at her little hand in mine, her sweet face gazing up at me to see if I liked her writing. I stumbled and almost fell, pretending to her that I'd tripped. As we walked around the room together, I looked down the entire time so none of the other parents could catch my eye and trigger a complete breakdown.

Milestone days were even more heart-wrenching. Dave had always made a big deal of the first day of school, taking lots of pictures as our kids went out the door. I tried to muster enthusiasm for taking those same pictures. The day of my daughter's birthday party, I sat on the floor of my bedroom with my mom, my sister, and Marne. I didn't think I could go downstairs and survive, much less smile through, a party. I knew I had to do it for my daughter. I also knew I had to do it for Dave. But I wanted to do it *with* Dave.

There were moments when even I could see some humor. While getting my hair cut, I mentioned that I was having trouble sleeping. My hairdresser put down his scissors and opened his bag with a flourish, pulling out Xanax in every possible shape and size. I declined—but really appreciated the gesture. One day I was on the phone complaining to my father that all the grief books had dreadful titles: *Death Is of Vital Importance* or *Say Yes to It*. (Like I could say no.) While we were on the phone a new one arrived, *Moving to the Center of the Bed*. Another day, on my drive home I turned on the radio to distract myself. Each song that came on was worse than the one before. "Somebody That I Used to Know." Awful. "Not the End." I beg to differ. "Forever Young." Not in this case. "Good Riddance: Time of Your Life." No and no. I finally settled on "Reindeer(s) Are Better than People."

My friend Davis Guggenheim told me that as a documentary filmmaker, he has learned to let the story reveal itself. He doesn't start each project knowing where the tale will end because it has to unfold in its own way and in its own time. Worried that I would try to control my grief, he encouraged me to listen to it, keep it close, and let it run its course. He knows me well. I searched for ways to end the sorrow, put it in a box, and throw it away. For the first weeks and months, I failed. The anguish won every time. Even when I looked calm and collected, the pain was always present. I was physically sitting in a meeting or reading to my kids, but my heart was on that gym floor.

"No one ever told me," C. S. Lewis wrote, "that grief felt so like fear." The fear was constant and it felt like the grief would never subside. The waves would continue to crash over me until I was no longer standing, no longer myself. In the worst of the void, two weeks after Dave died, I got a letter from an acquaintance in her sixties. She said that since she was ahead of me on this sad widow's path, she wished she had some good advice to offer, but she didn't. She had lost her husband a few years earlier, her close friend had lost hers a decade before, and neither of them felt that time had lessened the pain. She wrote, "Try as I might, I can't come up with a single thing that I know will help you." That letter, no doubt sent with the best of intentions, destroyed my hope that the pain would fade someday. I felt the void closing in on me, the years stretching before me endless and empty.

I called Adam Grant, a psychologist and professor at Wharton, and read the devastating letter to him. Two years earlier, Dave had read Adam's book *Give and Take* and invited him to speak at SurveyMonkey, where Dave was CEO. That evening, Adam joined us for dinner at our home. Adam studies how people find motivation and meaning, and we started talking about the challenges women face and how Adam's work could inform the issue. We began writing together and became friends. When Dave died, Adam flew across the country to attend the funeral. I confided to him that my greatest fear was that my kids would never be happy again. Other people had tried to reassure me with personal stories, but Adam walked me through the data: after losing a parent, many children are surprisingly resilient. They go on to have happy childhoods and become well-adjusted adults.

Hearing the despair in my voice triggered by the letter, Adam flew back across the country to convince me that there was a bottom to this seemingly endless void. He wanted to tell me face-to-face that while grief was unavoidable, there were things I could do to lessen the anguish for myself and my children. He said that by six months, more than half of people who lose a spouse are past what psychologists classify as "acute grief." Adam convinced me that while my grief would have to run its course, my beliefs and actions could shape how quickly I moved through the void and where I ended up.

I don't know anyone who has been handed only roses. We all encounter hardships. Some we see coming; others take us by surprise. It can be as tragic as the sudden death of a child, as heartbreaking as a relationship that unravels, or as disappointing as a dream that goes unfulfilled. The question is: When these things happen, what do we do next?

I thought resilience was the capacity to endure pain, so I asked Adam how I could figure out how much I had. He explained that our amount of resilience isn't fixed, so I should be asking instead how I could *become* resilient. Resilience is the strength and speed of our response to adversity—and we can build it. It isn't about having a backbone. It's about strengthening the muscles around our backbone.

Since Dave passed away, so many people have said to me, "I can't imagine." They mean they can't imagine this happening to them, can't imagine how I am standing there talking to them rather than curled up in a ball somewhere. I remember feeling the same way when I saw a colleague back at work after losing a child or a friend buying coffee after being diagnosed with cancer. When I was on the other side, my reply became, "I can't imagine either, but I have no choice."

I had no choice but to wake up every day. No choice but to get through the shock, the grief, the survivor guilt. No choice but to try to move forward and be a good mother at home. No choice but to try to focus and be a good colleague at work.

Loss, grief, and disappointment are profoundly personal. We all have unique circumstances and reactions to them. Still, the kindness and bravery of those who shared their experiences helped pull me through mine. Some who opened their hearts are my closest friends. Others are total strangers who offered wisdom and advice publicly—sometimes even in books with horrible titles. And Adam, patient yet insistent that the darkness would pass, but that I would have to help it along. That even in the face of the most shocking tragedy of my life, I could exert some control over its impact.

This book is my and Adam's attempt to share what we've learned about resilience. We wrote it together, but for simplicity and clarity the story is told by me (Sheryl) while Adam is referred to in the third person. We don't pretend that hope will win out over pain every day. It won't. We don't presume to have experienced every possible kind of loss and setback ourselves. We haven't. There is no right or proper way to grieve or face challenges, so we don't have perfect answers. There are no perfect answers.

We also know that not every story has a happy ending. For each hopeful story we tell here, there are others where circumstances were too much to overcome. Recovery does not start from the same place for everyone. Wars, violence, and systemic sexism and racism decimate lives and communities. Discrimination, disease, and poverty cause and worsen tragedy. The sad truth is that adversity is not evenly distributed among us; marginalized and disenfranchised groups have more to battle and more to grieve.

As traumatic as my family's experience has been, I'm well aware of how fortunate we are to have a wide support system of extended family, friends, and colleagues and access to financial resources that few have. I also know that talking about how to find strength in the face of hardship does not release us from the responsibility of working to prevent hardship in the first place. What we do in our communities and companies—the public policies we put in place, the ways we help one another—can ensure that fewer people suffer.

Yet try as we might to prevent adversity, inequality, and

trauma, they still exist and we are still left to cope with them. To fight for change tomorrow we need to build resilience today. Psychologists have studied how to recover and rebound from a wide range of adversity—from loss, rejection, and divorce to injury and illness, from professional failure to personal disappointment. Along with reviewing the research, Adam and I sought out individuals and groups who have overcome ordinary and extraordinary difficulties. Their stories changed the way we think about resilience.

This book is about the capacity of the human spirit to persevere. We look at the steps people can take, both to help themselves and to help others. We explore the psychology of recovery and the challenges of regaining confidence and rediscovering joy. We cover ways to speak about tragedy and comfort friends who are suffering. And we discuss what it takes to create resilient communities and companies, raise strong children, and love again.

I now know that it is possible to experience post-traumatic growth. In the wake of the most crushing blows, people can find greater strength and deeper meaning. I also believe that it is possible to experience *pre*-traumatic growth—that you don't have to experience tragedy to build your resilience for whatever lies ahead.

I am only partway through my own journey. The fog of acute grief has lifted, but the sadness and longing for Dave remain. I'm still finding my way through and learning many of the lessons included here. Like so many who've experienced tragedy, I hope I can choose meaning and even joy—and help others do the same.

Looking back over the darkest moments, I can now see that even then there were signs of hope. A friend reminded me that when my children broke down at the cemetery, I said to them, "This is the second worst moment of our lives. We lived through the first and we will live through this. It can only get better from here." Then I started singing a song I knew from childhood: "Oseh Shalom," a prayer for peace. I don't remember deciding to sing or how I picked this song. I later learned that it is the last line of the Kaddish, the Jewish prayer for mourning, which may explain why it poured out of me. Soon all the adults joined in, the children followed, and the wailing stopped. On my daughter's birthday, I did get off my bedroom floor and smile through her party, where to my total shock I saw that she was having a great time.

Just weeks after losing Dave, I was talking to Phil about a father-child activity. We came up with a plan for someone to fill in for Dave. I cried to Phil, "But I want Dave." He put his arm around me and said, "Option A is not available. So let's just kick the shit out of Option B."

Life is never perfect. We all live some form of Option B. This book is to help us all kick the shit out of it.

1

Breathing Again

You must go on,
I can't go on,
I'll go on.
—SAMUEL BECKETT

BOUT A YEAR AFTER Dave died, I was at work when my cell phone buzzed. An old friend was calling, and since nobody calls anyone anymore, I figured it must be important. It was. My friend had horrible news about a young woman she mentors. A few days earlier, the young woman had gone to a birthday party, and as she was leaving she noticed that a coworker needed a ride home. Since he lived nearby, she offered to drop him off. When they arrived, he pulled out a weapon, forced her inside, and raped her.

The young woman went to the hospital for a rape kit exam and then reported the attack to the police. Now my friend was looking for ways to provide comfort and knew I'd met this young woman, so she asked if I would talk with her and offer support. As I dialed her number, I felt nervous about whether

I'd be able to help someone recover from something so vio-
lent. But as I listened to her, I realized some of what I'd learned
about overcoming grief might resonate with her too.

We plant the seeds of resilience in the ways we process negative events. After spending decades studying how people deal
with setbacks, psychologist Martin Seligman found that three
P's can stunt recovery: (1) personalization—the belief that we
are at fault; (2) pervasiveness—the belief that an event will
affect all areas of our life; and (3) permanence—the belief that
the aftershocks of the event will last forever. The three P's play
like the flip side of the pop song "Everything Is Awesome"—
"everything is awful." The loop in your head repeats, "It's my
fault this is awful. My whole life is awful. And it's always going
to be awful."

Hundreds of studies have shown that children and adults
recover more quickly when they realize that hardships aren't
entirely their fault, don't affect every aspect of their lives, and
won't follow them everywhere forever. Recognizing that negative events aren't personal, pervasive, or permanent makes
people less likely to get depressed and better able to cope. Not
falling into the trap of the three P's helped teachers in urban
and rural schools: they were more effective in the classroom
and their students did better academically. It helped college varsity swimmers who underperformed in a race: their heart rates
spiked less and they went on to improve their times. And it
helped insurance salespeople in difficult jobs: when they didn't
take rejections personally and remembered that they could
approach new prospects tomorrow, they sold more than twice
as much and stayed in the job twice as long as their colleagues.

On my call with the young woman, at first I just listened as
she described how she felt violated, betrayed, angry, and scared.
Then she starting blaming herself, saying it was her fault for
giving her colleague a ride home. I encouraged her to stop per-

sonalizing the attack. Rape is never the victim's fault and offering a coworker a ride was a completely reasonable thing to do. I stressed that not everything that happens *to* us happens *because of* us. Then I brought up the two other P's: pervasiveness and permanence. We talked about all the good in other areas of her life and I encouraged her to think about how the despair would feel less acute with time.

Recovering from rape is an incredibly difficult and complicated process that differs for everyone. Evidence suggests that it's common for rape victims to blame themselves and feel hopeless about the future. Those who can break this pattern are at lower risk of depression and post-traumatic stress. A few weeks later, the young woman called to tell me that with her cooperation, the state was moving forward with prosecuting the rapist. She said she thought about the three P's every day and the advice had made her feel better. It had made me feel better too.

I'd fallen into these three traps myself, starting with personalization. I immediately blamed myself for Dave's death. The first medical report claimed that Dave had died of head trauma from falling off an exercise machine, so I worried incessantly that I could have saved him by finding him sooner. My brother David, a neurosurgeon, insisted that this was not true: falling from the height of a workout machine might break Dave's arm, but it wouldn't kill him. Something had happened to make Dave fall in the first place. The autopsy proved my brother right: Dave had died in a matter of seconds from a cardiac arrhythmia caused by coronary artery disease.

Even once I knew Dave had not died from neglect on a gym floor, I still found other reasons to blame myself. Dave's coronary artery disease was never diagnosed. I spent weeks with his doctors and the doctors in my family poring over his autopsy and medical records. I worried that he had complained of chest pain but we had missed it. I thought endlessly about his diet and if I should have pushed him to make more improvements. His doctors told me that no single lifestyle change would definitely have saved him. And it helped when Dave's family reminded me that his eating habits were much healthier whenever he was with me.

I also blamed myself for the disruption his death caused to everyone around me. Before this tragedy, I was the older sister, the doer, the planner, the leaner inner. But when Dave died, I was incapable of doing much of anything. Others jumped in to help. My boss Mark Zuckerberg, my brother-in-law Marc, and Marne planned the funeral. My father and sister-in-law Amy made the burial arrangements. When people came to pay their respects at our house, Amy nudged me to get up and thank them for coming. My father reminded me to eat and then sat next to me to make sure I actually did.

Over the next few months, the thing I found myself saying most often was, "I'm sorry." I apologized constantly to everyone. To my mom, who put her life on hold to stay with me for the first month. To my friends who dropped everything to travel to the funeral. To my clients for missing appointments. To my colleagues for losing focus when emotion overwhelmed me. I'd start a meeting thinking, *I can do this,* only to have tears well up, forcing a quick exit with a hasty "I'm so sorry." Not exactly the kind of disruption Silicon Valley is looking for.

Adam finally convinced me that I needed to banish the word "sorry." He also vetoed "I apologize," "I regret that," or any attempt to weasel my way past the ban. Adam explained that by blaming myself I was delaying my recovery, which also meant I was delaying my kids' recovery. That snapped me out of it. I realized that Dave's doctors had not prevented his death, so it was irrational for me to believe that I could have. I hadn't interrupted everyone's lives; tragedy had. No one thought I should apologize for crying. Once I tried to stop saying "sorry," I found myself biting my tongue over and over and started letting go of personalization.

As I blamed myself less, I started to notice that not *everything* was terrible. My son and daughter were sleeping through the night, crying less, and playing more. We had access to grief counselors and therapists. I could afford child care and support at home. I had loving family, friends, and colleagues; I marveled at how they were carrying me and my children—quite literally at times. I felt closer to them than I ever would have thought possible.

Going back to work helped with pervasiveness too. In the Jewish tradition, there is a seven-day intense mourning period known as shiva, after which most regular activities are supposed to resume. Child psychologists and grief experts counseled me to get my son and daughter back to their normal routines as soon as possible. So ten days after Dave passed away, they went back to school and I started going to work during school hours.

My first days back in the office were a complete haze. I had worked as the chief operating officer of Facebook for more than seven years but now everything felt unfamiliar. In my first meeting, all I could think was, *What is everyone talking about and why on earth does this even matter?* Then at one point I was drawn into the discussion and for a second—maybe half a second—I forgot. I forgot about death. I forgot the image of Dave lying on the gym floor. I forgot watching his casket being lowered into the ground. In my third meeting of the day, I actually fell asleep for a few minutes. As embarrassed as I was to find my head bobbing, I also felt grateful—and not just because I wasn't snoring. For the first time, I had relaxed. As the days turned into weeks and then months, I was able to concentrate for longer. Work gave me a place to feel more like myself, and the kindness of my colleagues showed me that not all aspects of my life were terrible.

I have long believed that people need to feel supported and understood at work. I now know that this is even more important after tragedy. And sadly, it's far less common than it should be. After the death of a loved one, only 60 percent of private sector workers get paid time off—and usually just a few days. When they return to work, grief can interfere with their job performance. The economic stress that frequently follows bereavement is like a one-two punch. In the United States alone, grief-related losses in productivity may cost companies as much as $75 billion annually. These losses could be decreased and the load could be lightened for people who are grieving if employers provided time off, flexible and reduced hours, and financial assistance. Companies that offer comprehensive health care, retirement, and family and medical leave benefits find that their long-term investment in employees pays off in a more loyal and productive workforce. Providing support is both the compassionate *and* the wise thing to do. I was grateful that Facebook offered generous bereavement leave, and after Dave died, I worked with our team to extend our policies even further.

The hardest of the three P's for me to process was permanence. For months, no matter what I did, I felt like the debilitating anguish would always be there. Most of the people I knew who had lived through tragedy said that over time the sadness subsides. They assured me that one day I would think of Dave and smile. I didn't believe them. When my children cried, I would flash forward to their entire lives without a father. Dave wasn't just going to miss a soccer game . . . but *all* the soccer games. *All* the debate tournaments. *All* the holidays. *All* the graduations. He would not walk our daughter down the aisle at her wedding. The fear of forever without Dave was paralyzing.

My dire projections put me in good company. When we're suffering, we tend to project it out indefinitely. Studies of "affective forecasting"—our predictions of how we'll feel in the future—reveal that we tend to overestimate how long negative events will affect us. Some students were asked to imagine their current romantic relationship ending and predict how unhappy they'd feel two months later. Other students were asked to report their own happiness two months after an *actual* breakup. Those who experienced a real split were far happier than expected. People also overestimate the negative impact of other stressful events. Assistant professors thought being denied university tenure would leave them despondent for the next five years. It didn't. College students believed they would be miserable if they got stuck in an undesirable dorm. They weren't. As someone who was assigned to the least desirable dorm in my college—twice—this study rings especially true.

Just as the body has a physiological immune system, the brain has a psychological immune system. When something goes wrong, we instinctively marshal defense mechanisms. We see silver linings in clouds. We add sugar and water to lemons. We start clinging to clichés. But after losing Dave, I wasn't able to do any of this. Every time I tried to tell myself things would get better, a louder voice inside my head insisted that they would not. It seemed clear that my children and I would never have another moment of pure joy again. *Never.*

Seligman found that words like "never" and "always" are signs of permanence. Just as I had to banish "sorry" from my vocabulary, I tried to eliminate "never" and "always" and replace them with "sometimes" and "lately." "I will *always* feel this awful" became "I will *sometimes* feel this awful." Not the most cheerful thought, but still an improvement. I noticed that there were moments when the pain temporarily eased up, like a splitting headache that briefly dulls. As I had more reprieves,

I was able to recall them when I sank back into deeper grief. I started to learn that no matter how sad I felt, another break would eventually come. It helped me regain a sense of control.

I also tried a cognitive behavioral therapy technique where you write down a belief that's causing you anguish and then follow it with proof that the belief is false. I started with my biggest fear: "My children will never have a happy childhood." Staring at that sentence on paper made my stomach turn but also made me realize that I had spoken with many people who had lost parents at a young age and went on to prove that prediction wrong. Another time I wrote, "I will never feel okay again." Seeing those words forced me to realize that just that morning, someone had told a joke and I had laughed. If only for one minute, I'd already proven that sentence false.

A psychiatrist friend explained to me that humans are evolutionarily wired for both connection and grief: we naturally have the tools to recover from loss and trauma. That helped me believe that I could get through this. If we had evolved to handle suffering, the deep grief would not kill me. I thought about how humans had faced love and loss for centuries, and I felt connected to something much larger than myself—connected to a universal human experience. I reached out to one of my favorite professors, Reverend Scotty McLennan, who had kindly counseled me in my twenties when my first husband and I divorced. Now Scotty explained that in his forty years of helping people through loss, he has seen that "turning to God gives people a sense of being enveloped in loving arms that are eternal and ultimately strong. People need to know that they are not alone."

Thinking about these connections helped, yet I couldn't shake the overpowering sense of dread. Memories and images of Dave were everywhere. In those first few months, I'd wake up every morning and experience the sickening realization that he was still gone. At night, I'd walk into the kitchen expecting to see him, and when he wasn't there the pain hit hard. Mark Zuckerberg and his wife Priscilla Chan thought it might be comforting to take me and my kids to a place where we had no memories of Dave, so they invited us to join them on a beach we'd never seen. Yet when I sat on a bench overlooking the ocean, I glanced into the big open sky . . . and saw Dave's face looking down on me from the clouds. I was sitting between Mark and Priscilla and I could feel their arms around me, but somehow Dave managed to be there too.

There was no escape. My grief felt like a deep, thick fog that constantly surrounded me. My friend Kim Jabal, who had lost her brother, described it as a lead blanket covering her face and body. Dave's brother Rob said it felt like there was a boot pushing down on his chest that made it nearly impossible to get air into his lungs, one pressing even harder than when their father had died sixteen years before. I had trouble filling my lungs too. My mom taught me how to breathe through the waves of anxiety: breathe in for a count of six, hold my breath for a count of six, then exhale for a count of six. My goddaughter Elise, in a touching reversal of our relationship, held my hand and counted aloud with me until the panic subsided.

Rabbi Nat Ezray, who led Dave's funeral, told me to "lean in to the suck"—to expect it to be awful. Not exactly what I meant when I said "lean in," but for me it was good advice. Years earlier, I'd noticed that when I got sad or anxious, often the second derivative of those feelings made them doubly upsetting. When I felt down, I also felt down that I was down. When I felt anxious, I felt anxious that I was anxious. "Part of every misery," C. S. Lewis wrote, is "misery's shadow . . . the fact that you don't merely suffer but have to keep on thinking about the fact that you suffer."

Following Dave's death, I had stronger second-derivative

negative feelings than ever before. I wasn't just grief-stricken; I was grief-stricken that I was grief-stricken. I wasn't just anxious; I was meta-anxious. Small things that never really concerned me before, like the possibility of my kids getting injured riding their bikes to school, worried me incessantly. Then I worried that I was overworrying. Taking my rabbi's advice and accepting that this completely sucked helped a great deal. Instead of being surprised by the negative feelings, I expected them.

A friend told me I had just learned something Buddhists have known since the fifth century BC. The first noble truth of Buddhism is that all life involves suffering. Aging, sickness, and loss are inevitable. And while life includes some joyful moments, despite our attempts to make them last, they too will dissolve. Buddhist teacher Pema Chödrön, who broke the Zen ceiling as the first American woman to become fully ordained in the Tibetan tradition, writes that when we accept this noble truth, it actually lessens our pain because we end up "making friends with our own demons." I wasn't going out for a drink with my demons, but as I accepted them, they did haunt me less.

A few days after Dave's funeral, my son and daughter and I made a list of our new "family rules" and hung it over the cubbies where they put their backpacks so we'd see it every day. Rule number one was "Respect our feelings." We discussed how the sadness might come over them at awkward times, like during school, and that when it did, they could take a break from whatever they were doing. Their cry breaks were frequent and their teachers kindly arranged for them to go outside with a friend or to the guidance counselor so they could let their feelings out.

I gave this advice to my kids but also had to take it myself. Leaning in to the suck meant admitting that I could not control when the sadness would come over me. I needed cry breaks too.

I took them on the side of the road in my car . . . at work . . . at board meetings. Sometimes I went to the women's room to sob and sometimes I just cried at my desk. When I stopped fighting those moments, they passed more quickly.

After a few months, I started to notice that the fog of intense pain lifted now and then, and when it rolled back in, I recovered faster. It occurred to me that dealing with grief was like building physical stamina: the more you exercise, the faster your heart rate recovers after it is elevated. And sometimes during especially vigorous physical activity, you discover strength you didn't know you had.

Shockingly, one of the things that helped me the most was focusing on worst-case scenarios. Predicting a bad situation was usually easy for me; it's a fine old Jewish tradition, like rejecting the first table offered in a restaurant. But during the early days of despair, my instinct was to try to find positive thoughts. Adam told me the opposite: that it was a good idea to think about how much worse things could be. "Worse?" I asked him. "Are you kidding? How could this be worse?" His answer cut through me: "Dave could have had that same cardiac arrhythmia driving your children." *Wow.* The thought that I could have lost all three of them had never occurred to me. I instantly felt overwhelmingly grateful that my children were alive and healthy—and that gratitude overtook some of the grief.

Dave and I had a family ritual at dinner where we'd go around the table with our daughter and son and take turns stating our best and worst moments of the day. When it became just three of us, I added a third category. Now we each share something for which we are grateful. We also added a prayer before our meal. Holding hands and thanking God for the food we are about to eat helps remind us of our daily blessings.

Acknowledging blessings can be a blessing in and of itself.

Psychologists asked a group of people to make a weekly list of five things for which they were grateful. Another group wrote about hassles and a third listed ordinary events. Nine weeks later, the gratitude group felt significantly happier and reported fewer health problems. People who enter the workforce during an economic recession end up being more satisfied with their jobs decades later because they are acutely aware of how hard it can be to find work. Counting blessings can actually increase happiness and health by reminding us of the good things in life. Each night, no matter how sad I felt, I would find something or someone to be grateful for.

I also deeply appreciated our financial security. Both my daughter and my son asked me if we were going to have to move out of our house. I knew how lucky we were that the answer was no. For many, an unexpected event like a single hospital visit or a car repair can undo financial stability overnight. In the European Union, one in four people are at risk of poverty—and this risk is heightened for women and single parents. Sixty percent of Americans have faced an event that threatened their ability to make ends meet and a third have no savings, which leaves them constantly vulnerable. The death of a partner often brings severe financial consequences—especially for women, who frequently earn less than men and have less access to retirement benefits. In addition to the devastation of losing a beloved partner, widows are often left without money for basic needs and lose their homes. Of the 258 million widows across the world, more than 115 million live in poverty. This is one of many reasons why it's important to erase the wage gap for women.

We need to embrace all families regardless of the different forms they take and provide the help they need to get through the hardships they face. Cohabiting and same-sex couples usually don't have the same legal protections and employment benefits as married couples. We need stronger social insurance policies and more family-friendly business practices to prevent tragedy from leading to more hardship. Single parents and widows deserve more support, and leaders, coworkers, families, and neighbors can commit to providing it.

Even being aware of all my blessings, I was still consumed by the pain. Four months and two days after I found Dave on the floor, I attended my kids' Back to School Night. For the first time, I drove there alone. Parents gathered in the gym and then headed into their children's individual classrooms. Dave and I had always split up to cover our son's and daughter's classes and compared notes later. Man-to-man defense. Not anymore.

I'd been dreading choosing a classroom all week, and when that moment came a wave of sadness engulfed me. I was walking toward the rooms, holding my friend Kim's hand while trying to decide, when my phone rang. It was my doctor. He said that he wanted to reach me right away because a routine mammogram had revealed a suspicious spot. My heart raced. He told me that there was no need to worry yet—*very helpful*—but that I should come in the next day for an ultrasound.

My sadness turned to panic. Rather than go to either classroom, I got in my car and fled home. Since losing their father, my children had been understandably obsessed with death. At dinner a few weeks earlier, my daughter needed a cry break and I followed her into her room. I curled up beside her on the bed and she reached for my necklace, which had dangling charms of our family's four initials. She said with determination, "I'm going to pick one." I asked her why. She said she wouldn't tell me because I'd get upset. I told her she could say anything. In a whisper, she explained, "The one I pick will die next." I felt the breath escape from my lungs. Somehow, I held it together and said, "Then let me pick." I selected the "S" and said, "I will be the next to die—and I think it will be in forty years when I am over ninety." I didn't know if that was the right thing to say (and my math was wrong) but I wanted to comfort her.

As I drove home from Back to School Night, I felt her hand as if it were tugging on my necklace. *How could I ever tell her and my son that I had cancer?* And what if—*what if*—they lost me too? And how was it possible that a few minutes ago I was so stressed over which classroom to choose?

That evening, I was shaking and sobbing too much to put my kids to bed. I didn't want to upset them, so my mother tucked them in. My sister came over and the three of us held hands and prayed. I couldn't think of anything else to do. My mom said a few words in prayer and I asked her to repeat them again and again and again.

The next seventeen hours crawled by. I couldn't sleep, eat, or carry on a coherent conversation. I just watched the clock, waiting for my one p.m. appointment.

The ultrasound showed that the mammogram result had been a false positive. The gratitude that flooded my entire body was as overwhelming as the grief I had felt over the past four endless months. In one fell swoop, I felt more appreciation for my health and what was good in my life than I ever had before.

Looking back, I wish I had known about the three P's earlier. There were so many times they would have helped, even with daily challenges. On the first day of my first job out of college, my boss asked me to enter data into Lotus 1-2-3—a popular spreadsheet in the 1990s. I had to admit that I didn't know how. His mouth dropped open and he said, "I can't believe you got this job without knowing that." Then he walked out of the room. I went home convinced that I was going to be fired. I thought I was terrible at everything, but it turns out I was only terrible at spreadsheets. Understanding pervasiveness would have saved me a lot of anxiety that week. And I wish somebody had told me about permanence when I broke up with boyfriends. I could have avoided a lot of angst if I'd known that the heartache was not going to last forever—and if I was really being honest with myself, neither were any of those relationships. I also wish I had known about personalization when boyfriends broke up with me. (Sometimes it's not you—it really *is* them.)

All three P's ganged up on me in my twenties after my first marriage ended in divorce. I thought at the time that no matter what I accomplished, I would always be a massive failure. Looking back, it was that failed marriage that led me to leave D.C. and move across the country to Los Angeles, where I barely knew anyone. Fortunately, one of my friends invited me to join him and his buddy for dinner and a movie. That night, the three of us went to a deli, then saw *Courage Under Fire*, where I fell asleep on Dave's shoulder for the first time.

We all deal with loss: jobs lost, loves lost, lives lost. The question is not whether these things will happen. They will, and we will have to face them.

Resilience comes from deep within us and from support outside us. It comes from gratitude for what's good in our lives and from leaning in to the suck. It comes from analyzing how we process grief and from simply accepting that grief. Sometimes we have less control than we think. Other times we have more.

I learned that when life pulls you under, you can kick against the bottom, break the surface, and breathe again.

2

Kicking the Elephant
Out of the Room

"*No, this is the elephant.*"

IN COLLEGE, most people have a roommate or two. Some have three or four. Dave had ten. After graduation, the roommates scattered across the country, seeing one another only on special occasions. In the spring of 2014, we all got together for their twenty-fifth college reunion. The families had so much fun that we decided to spend the Fourth of July together the next year.

Dave passed away two months before the trip.

I thought about skipping it. The prospect of spending the weekend with Dave's roommates *without Dave* seemed overwhelmingly hard. But I was grasping to hang on to the life we had together, and canceling felt like giving up another piece of him. So I went, hoping that it would be comforting to be with his close friends, who were also grieving.

Most of the trip was a blur, but on the last day, I sat down for breakfast with several of the roommates, including Jeff King, who had been diagnosed years earlier with multiple sclerosis. Dave and I had discussed Jeff's illness many times with each other, but that morning I realized that I had never actually spoken with Jeff about it.

Hello, Elephant.

"Jeff," I said, "how are you? I mean, really, how are you? How are you feeling? Are you scared?"

Jeff looked up in surprise and paused for a long few moments. With tears in his eyes, he said, "Thank you. Thank you for asking." And then he talked. He talked about his diagnosis and how he hated that he had to stop practicing medicine. How his continued deterioration was hard on his children. How he was worried about his future. How relieved he felt being able to talk about it with me and the others at the table that morning. When breakfast was over, he hugged me tight.

In the early weeks after Dave died, I was shocked when I'd see friends who did not ask how I was doing. The first time it happened, I thought I was dealing with a non-question-asking friend. We all have some of these, as blogger Tim Urban describes them: "You'll quit your job. You'll fall in love. You'll catch your new love cheating on you and murder them both in

an act of incredible passion. And it doesn't matter, because none
of it will be discussed with The Non-Question-Asking Friend,
who never, ever, ever asks you anything about your life." Sometimes these friends are self-absorbed. Sometimes they're just
uncomfortable having intimate conversations.

I couldn't understand when friends didn't ask me how I
was. I felt invisible, as if I were standing in front of them but
they couldn't see me. When someone shows up with a cast,
we immediately inquire, "What happened?" If your ankle gets
shattered, people ask to hear the story. If your life gets shattered, they don't.

People continually avoided the subject. I went to a close
friend's house for dinner, and she and her husband made small
talk the entire time. I listened mystified, keeping my thoughts
to myself. *You're right, the Warriors are totally crushing it! And you
know who really loved that team? Dave.* I got emails from friends
asking me to fly to their cities to speak at their events without acknowledging that travel might be more difficult for me
now. *Oh, it's just an overnight? Sure, I'll see if Dave can come back
to life and put the kids to bed.* I ran into friends at local parks who
talked about the weather. *Yes! The weather has been weird with all
this rain and death.*

It wasn't until breakfast with Jeff that I realized I was sometimes the friend who avoided painful conversations. I had failed
to ask him directly about his health not because I didn't care,
but because I was worried about upsetting him. Losing Dave
taught me how ludicrous that was. It wasn't possible for me to
remind Jeff that he was living with MS. He was aware of that
every minute of every day.

Even people who have endured the worst suffering often
want to talk about it. Merle Saferstein is one of my mom's
closest friends and the former education director at the Holocaust Documentation and Education Center in South Florida.

She has worked with more than five hundred survivors and remembers only one who declined to open up. "In my experience, survivors want the opportunity to teach and not be shunned because they went through something unknowable," Merle said. Still, people hesitate to ask questions out of concern that probing will dredge up trauma. To encourage discussion, Merle ran programs that brought survivors together with high school and college students. She notes that when students are offered the chance, questions tumble out. "I've heard them inquire, 'What did you eat in the concentration camp? Did you still believe in God?' Young girls will often ask, 'Did you get your period? What did you do when you did?' These aren't personal questions. They are human questions," Merle told me.

Avoiding feelings isn't the same as protecting feelings. Merle recalled going with a young cousin of hers to visit an elderly couple who had clay handprints of two children hanging on their wall. The couple spoke of only one daughter. Merle's young cousin had been told not to mention their daughter who died because it would make the couple sad. Merle hadn't heard this warning, so she asked about the second set of prints. While the cousin looked aghast, the couple spoke warmly and at length about their daughter. "They wanted her to be remembered," Merle said.

Parents who have suffered the worst loss imaginable often share this sentiment. Author Mitch Carmody said after his nine-year-old son Kelly died from a brain tumor, "Our child dies a second time when no one speaks their name." This is why the Compassionate Friends, one of the largest bereavement organizations in the United States, encourages families to speak openly and frequently about the children they have lost.

Avoiding upsetting topics is so common that the practice even has a name. Decades ago, psychologists coined the term "mum effect" for when people avoid sharing bad news.

Doctors hold back on telling patients that their prognosis is bleak. Managers wait too long to break the news that people are being fired. My colleague Maxine Williams, head of diversity at Facebook, told me that she believes many people succumb to the mum effect around race. "Even after an unarmed black person is killed for reaching over to show a cop his license, white people who have seen the news, who live in these communities, and who sit at the desk next to us at work will often say nothing," Maxine said. "For the victim of racism, like the victim of loss, the silence is crippling. The two things we want to know when we're in pain are that we're not crazy to feel the way we do and that we have support. Acting like nothing significant is happening to people who look like us denies us all of that."

By staying silent, we often isolate family, friends, and coworkers. Even under ordinary circumstances, being alone with your thoughts can be uncomfortable. In one experiment, a quarter of women and two-thirds of men chose to give themselves painful electric shocks rather than sit in solitude for fifteen minutes. Silence can increase suffering. I only felt comfortable bringing up Dave with a small group of family and friends. Some of my other friends and coworkers made it easy for me to open up; psychologists literally call them "openers." Unlike non-question-asking friends, openers ask a lot of questions and listen to the answers without judging. They enjoy learning about and feeling connected to others. Openers can make a big difference in times of crisis, especially for those who are normally reticent.

I never would've expected that I'd have trouble sharing. With my close friends, I'm always the one who wants to talk about everything. *Do you like him? Is he a good kisser?* (Not always in that order.) At work, I constantly ask for feedback—to the point that I get feedback that I ask for too much feedback. But in grief, I didn't want to dump my problems on others and was unable to mention Dave unless people really pressed.

Openers are not always our closest friends. People who have faced adversity tend to express more compassion toward others who are suffering. Writer Anna Quindlen observes that grief is discussed among "those of us who recognize in one another a kindred chasm deep in the center of who we are." Military veterans, rape victims, and parents whose children have died all report that the most helpful support usually comes from those who have suffered similar losses. When Holocaust survivors came to the United States, Merle told me, "they felt very isolated, so they started bonding with each other. That's why the survivor clubs formed. The only people who really understood were the people who had been through those experiences."

I found this to be true. Colin Summers, a friend from Los Angeles, approached me at Dave's funeral. Instead of saying, "I'm sorry for your loss," the first thing out of his mouth was, "My dad died when I was four." "Oh, good," I blurted in response. Then I quickly added, "I mean, not *good*. It's just that you turned out great and that gives me hope for my children." I was embarrassed, but he gave me a hug and said, "I knew what you meant and I promise your kids are stronger than you know." It wasn't my smoothest social interaction, but it was one of the only moments on that horrible day that made me feel a tiny bit better.

I had become a member of a club that no one wants to belong to—a club that I did not even know existed before I joined involuntarily. Nine days after Dave died, I went to my daughter's soccer game and noticed her friend's seventy-year-old grandmother, Jo Shepherd, sitting next to an empty chair.

Decades before, Jo had also been left to raise two small children when her husband died, and I instinctively knew that chair was for me. I sat down, and before we'd said ten words to each other I felt completely understood. At a Facebook partner breakfast, a client I'd never met before told me that he had just lost his brother. We wound up sitting in the corner and crying together.

Many people who had not experienced loss, even some very close friends, didn't know what to say to me or my kids. Their discomfort being around us was palpable, especially in contrast to our previous ease. As the elephant in the room went unacknowledged, it started acting up, trampling over my relationships. If friends didn't ask how I was doing, did that mean they didn't care? Did they not see the giant muddy footprints and piles of manure?

Adam was certain people wanted to talk about it but they didn't know how. I was less sure. Friends were asking, "How are you?" but I took this as more of a standard greeting than a genuine question. I wanted to scream back, "My husband just died, how do you think I am?" I didn't know how to respond to pleasantries. *Aside from that, how was the play, Mrs. Lincoln?*

All over the world, there is cultural pressure to conceal negative emotions. In China and Japan, the ideal emotional state is calm and composed. In the United States, we like excitement (OMG!) and enthusiasm (LOL!). As psychologist David Caruso observes, "American culture demands that the answer to the question 'How are you?' is not just 'Good.' . . . We need to be 'Awesome.'" Caruso adds, "There's this relentless drive to mask the expression of our true underlying feelings." Admitting that you're having a rough time is "almost inappropriate."

Anna Quindlen puts it more poetically. "Grief," she writes, is "a whisper in the world and a clamor within. More than sex, more than faith, even more than its usher death, grief is unspoken, publicly ignored except for those moments at the funeral that are over too quickly."

The elephant followed me to the office too. I've always been friendly with my colleagues, especially at Facebook, where our company mission is to make the world more open and connected. Our culture reflects this: all of us sit at open desks where anyone can walk up and talk to anyone else. Conversations, including personal ones, are frequent and public.

At first, going back to work provided a bit of a sense of normalcy. Then I quickly discovered that it wasn't business as usual. I have long encouraged people to bring their whole selves to work, but now my "whole self" was just so freaking sad. As hard as it was to bring up Dave with friends, it seemed even more inappropriate at work. So I did not. And they did not. Most of my interactions felt cold, distant, stilted. Walking around the Facebook campus, I started to feel like a ghost, somehow frightening and invisible at the same time. In the moments when I couldn't take it, I sought refuge with Mark in his conference room. I told him I was worried that my personal connections with our coworkers were slipping away. He understood my fear but insisted that I was misreading their reactions. He said they wanted to stay close to me but they did not know what to say.

The deep loneliness of my loss was compounded by so many distancing daily interactions that I started to feel worse and worse. I thought about carrying around a stuffed elephant but I wasn't sure that anyone would get the hint. I knew that people were doing their best; those who said nothing were trying not to bring on more pain, and those who said the wrong thing were trying to comfort. I saw myself in many of these attempts—they were doing exactly what I had done when I was on the other side. With the best of intentions, if friends were in pain, I had tried to offer optimism and reassurance to minimize their fears. *Yep, I see a gray animal in the room, but that's no elephant—looks more like a mouse.* I now realize that it was just wishful thinking on my part that could make people feel even less understood.

The traditional Jewish period of mourning for a spouse lasts thirty days. I was nearing the end of the month when I thought about expressing how I felt on Facebook. I poured my emotions into a post but didn't think I'd ever share it—it was too personal, too raw, too revealing. Finally, I decided it was unlikely to make things worse and maybe it would make them a bit better. Early the next morning before I could change my mind, I hit "post."

My message began by describing the void and how easy it was to get sucked in. I said that for the first time ever, I understood the power of the prayer "Let me not die while I am still alive." Grasping for a lifeline, I wrote about how I wanted to choose meaning over emptiness. I thanked my family and friends who had helped me through those incomprehensible first weeks. Then I did what proved so difficult to do with friends and colleagues face-to-face: I described how a casual greeting like "How are you?" hurt because it didn't acknowledge that anything out of the ordinary had happened. I pointed out that if people instead asked "How are you today?" it showed that they were aware that I was struggling to get through each day.

The impact of my post was immediate. Friends, neighbors, and colleagues started talking about the elephant. Emails poured in with messages like "I know it must be really hard. I've been thinking about you and your kids."

The responses from strangers around the world made me feel less isolated too. A new mother wrote from a hospital neonatal intensive care unit that she'd lost one of her newborn twins and sought the strength to give the surviving twin an amazing life. A young man shared his wedding photo the day before what would have been his third anniversary. His late wife had changed his world, and he promised that in her memory he would help women succeed in his male-dominated field. Strangers comforted each other. To the mother who lost her newborn twin, a woman who'd experienced the same thing offered solace. To the young widower, dozens of people wrote messages of encouragement. And in many cases, friends commented to friends that they had not known about their losses and wanted to be there to support them. Some offered compassion, others shared personal stories, but the message was clear: as one man wrote, even though Option A was gone for so many of us, we were not alone.

Not everyone feels comfortable talking openly about personal tragedy. We all make our own choices about when and where and if we want to express our feelings. Still, there's powerful evidence that opening up about traumatic events can improve mental and physical health. Speaking to a friend or family member often helps people understand their own emotions and feel understood.

After my post, one welcome change was that people began asking, "How are you *today*?" which became a shorthand way to express empathy. That question also helped me realize that my all-encompassing grief might not be permanent. Adam pointed out that I would often answer "How are you?" with "Fine," and that didn't encourage people to ask further questions. He said if I wanted others to be more open with me, I needed to be more open with them. I started responding more frankly. "I'm not fine, and it's nice to be able to be honest about that with you." I learned that even small things could let people know that I needed help; when they hugged me hello, if I hugged them just a bit tighter, they understood that I was not okay.

With a few of my non-question-asking friends, I addressed

our situation directly. I gathered my courage and told them, usually through tears, that when they didn't ask, I sometimes felt like they didn't care. I was grateful that they all reacted with kindness, saying they appreciated my speaking up—and they started asking more questions. Just like I had with Dave's college roommate Jeff, they had been inquiring, "How are you?" with a genuine desire to connect, but I hadn't given a true response and they didn't feel comfortable pushing for one.

I finally figured out that since the elephant was following me around, I could take the first step in acknowledging its existence. At work, I told my closest colleagues that they could ask me questions—any questions—and they could talk about how they felt too. One colleague said he was paralyzed when I was around, worried he might say the wrong thing. Another admitted she'd been driving by my house frequently, not sure if she should knock on the door. Once I told her that I wanted to talk to her, she finally rang the doorbell and came inside. I was happy to see her . . . and not just because she brought Starbucks.

There were times I wanted to avoid real conversations: In front of my son and daughter. Right before a meeting. What worked best for me was when people said, "I'm here if you ever want to talk. Like now. Or later. Or in the middle of the night. Whatever would help you." Instead of making assumptions about whether or not someone wants to talk, it's best to offer an opening and see if they take it.

Death is not the only kind of adversity that summons the elephant. Anything that reminds us of the possibility of loss can leave us at a loss for words. Financial difficulties. Divorce. Unemployment. Rape. Addiction. Incarceration. Illness. Adam told me that ten years ago, the day before he and his wife Allison were supposed to move to England for a fellowship, she had a miscarriage. They considered canceling their plans but thought that a change of scenery might be a good way to heal. Because of the distance and their fear of burdening others, they didn't tell friends and family about the miscarriage—or the second one that followed. It was then that Allison, who has a background in psychiatry, taught Adam that when something terrible happens, it can be important to consider how things could be worse. They remembered that a close friend had seven miscarriages before having healthy children. They thought about how losses later in pregnancy can be far more devastating. When they returned home, the pain was less raw and it was easier to talk about. Allison started sharing her experiences with her friends and found out that several of them had suffered the same loss but never said a word either.

Speaking up can strengthen social bonds, but in some cases it's risky. Having been one of the few Filipinos on his college campus, Anthony Ocampo described to us how he felt "the pressure of the American dream—to be the representative of the people in our community." He was also carrying an additional weight that he kept to himself: "For the hard-core Catholic Filipino immigrants that my parents were, having a gay son was never part of the plan." Anthony became a sociology professor and studied the challenges of coming out in immigrant families. He conducted interviews and learned about a Filipino teenager who drank from a cup and then watched his mother "throw it away because she thought it was dirty." When another immigrant son came out to his family, they drove him to Mexico and "took away his passport so he could learn to be a man."

Anthony saw the paradox of immigrant parents knowing the pain of exclusion yet inflicting that same pain on their LGBTQ children. When Anthony finally told his parents he was gay, he also shared with them the research he'd done on the damage caused when families turn away from their own. "The children look for acceptance in drugs, alcohol, and unsafe sex," he told them. "They remember it for years, and it affects pretty much every aspect of their lives." With Anthony's thoughtful and patient encouragement, his parents were able to accept him. Now they include Anthony's partner in their holiday celebrations. Breaking the silence brought them closer together.

Cancer is another forbidden or "whisper" topic. I read about a writer named Emily McDowell who said the worst part of being diagnosed with lymphoma wasn't feeling sick from chemo or losing her hair. "It was the loneliness and isolation I felt when many of my close friends and family members disappeared because they didn't know what to say, or said the absolute wrong thing without realizing it." In response, Emily created "empathy cards." I love them all but these two are my favorites, making me want to laugh and cry simultaneously.

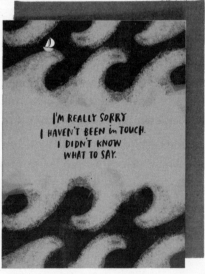

When I first read Emily's cards, I thought back to a friend with late-stage cancer telling me that for him the worst thing people could say was, "It's going to be okay." He said the terrified voice in his head would wonder, *How do you know it is going to be okay? Don't you understand that I might die?* I remembered the year before Dave died when a friend of mine was diagnosed with cancer. At the time, I thought the best way to offer comfort was to assure her, "You'll be okay. I just know it." Then I dropped the subject for weeks, thinking she would raise it again if she wanted to.

I meant well then, but I know better now. Recently, a work colleague was diagnosed with cancer and I handled it differently. I told her, "I know you don't know yet what will happen—and neither do I. But you won't go through this alone. I will be there with you every step of the way." By saying this, I acknowledged that she was in a stressful and scary situation. I then continued to check in with her regularly.

Sometimes, despite the best intentions, we still get it wrong. ABC News anchor Diane Sawyer had just returned to work after her husband Mike Nichols died. Diane was riding up an escalator when a colleague on the way down shouted out, "Sorry for your loss!" On the plus side, they were moving in opposite directions so she didn't have to respond.

"When you're faced with tragedy, you usually find that you're no longer surrounded by people—you're surrounded by platitudes. So what do we offer instead of 'everything happens for a reason'?" asks writer Tim Lawrence. He suggests that "the most powerful thing you can do is acknowledge. To literally say the words: I acknowledge your pain. I'm here with you."

Until we acknowledge it, the elephant is always there. By ignoring it, those who are grieving isolate themselves and those who could offer comfort create distance instead. Both sides need to reach out. Speaking with empathy and honesty is a good place to start. You can't wish the elephant away, but you can say, "I see it. I see you're suffering. And I care about you." Ideally not shouted from an escalator.

"I'm right there in the room, and no one even acknowledges me."

3

The Platinum Rule of Friendship

O NE AUGUST MORNING during Adam's first semester
teaching in Philadelphia, a student lumbered into his
classroom. At six foot two and 240 pounds, Owen
Thomas had been recruited to play defensive lineman on the
University of Pennsylvania football team. But size wasn't the
only thing that made Owen instantly command attention. His
hair was so orange that from a distance it looked like his head
was on fire. Adam would have noticed Owen even if he'd sat in
the back row, but he sat right in front, always arriving early and
asking insightful questions.

Owen made each of his classmates feel welcome, introducing himself with a friendly grin. During a unit on negotiations,
students divided into pairs to buy or sell a fictional business.
Owen finished with the worst results in the class. He couldn't
bear to take even a dime of hypothetical money that he didn't
need, so he practically gave his business away. In December,
when his classmates voted on who was the most cooperative
negotiator, Owen won in a landslide.

In April, he died by suicide.

Just two months earlier, Owen had stopped by Adam's office to ask for help. Owen was always upbeat, but that day he seemed anxious. He said he was looking for an internship and Adam offered to make a few introductions. Owen never followed up and that was the last time they spoke. Looking back on that meeting, Adam felt that he had failed when it mattered most. After the funeral, Adam went home and asked his wife Allison if he should quit teaching.

An autopsy revealed that Owen's brain showed signs of chronic traumatic encephalopathy (CTE), a disease believed to be caused in part by repeated hits to the head. CTE has been linked to severe depression and implicated in the suicides of a number of football players. At the time of his death, Owen was the youngest player to be diagnosed and the first with no history of concussions. After learning about the CTE diagnosis, Adam blamed himself less for missing the warning signs of mental illness and started thinking about ways to give more support to students who were struggling. But with hundreds of new students each fall, Adam needed a way to make a personal connection with many people at once. He drew his inspiration from a burst of noise.

In classic experiments on stress, people performed tasks that required concentration, like solving puzzles, while being blasted at random intervals with uncomfortably loud sounds. They started sweating and their heart rates and blood pressure climbed. They struggled to focus and made mistakes. Many got so frustrated that they gave up. Searching for a way to reduce anxiety, researchers gave some of the participants an escape. If the noise became too unpleasant, they could press a button and make it stop. Sure enough, the button allowed them to stay calmer, make fewer mistakes, and show less irritation. That's not surprising. But here's what is: *none of the participants actually pressed the button*. Stopping the noise didn't make the difference . . . knowing they *could* stop the noise did. The button gave them a sense of control and allowed them to endure the stress.

When people are in pain, they need a button. After Owen's suicide, Adam started writing his cell phone number on the board on the first day of his undergraduate class. He lets his students know that if they need him, they can call at any hour. Students use the number infrequently, but along with the mental health resources available on campus, this gives them each an extra button.

When people close to us face adversity, how do we give them a button to press? While it seems obvious that friends want to support friends going through a crisis, there are barriers that block us. There are two different emotional responses to the pain of others: empathy, which motivates us to help, and distress, which motivates us to avoid. Writer Allen Rucker observed both reactions after being suddenly paralyzed by a rare disorder. "As some friends checked in daily with deli sandwiches, the complete films of Alfred Hitchcock, or just kindness, others were curiously absent," he wrote. "It was my first indication that my new condition could breed fear in people other than myself." For some, his physical paralysis triggered emotional paralysis.

When we hear that someone we care about has lost a job, started chemo, or is going through a divorce, our first impulse is usually "I should reach out." Then right after that impulse doubts often flood our mind. "What if I say the wrong thing?" "What if talking about it makes her feel self-conscious?" "What if I'm overstepping?" Once raised, these doubts are followed by excuses like "He has so many friends and we're not *that* close." Or "She must be so busy. I don't want to bother her." We put off calling or offering help until we feel guilty that we didn't do it sooner . . . and then it feels too late.

A woman I know lost her husband to cancer in her fifties. Before this tragedy, she used to speak to one of her friends every week; then, suddenly, the calls stopped. Almost a year later, the widow picked up the phone. "Why haven't I heard from you?" she asked. "Oh," explained her friend, "I wanted to wait until you felt better." Her friend didn't understand that withholding comfort actually added to the pain.

Alycia Bennett was on the receiving end of the distress response when she needed comfort most. In high school, Alycia ran a local chapter of a nonprofit to fight poverty in Africa, and she arrived at college eager to continue this mission. She contacted an administrator involved with non-profits on campus, who came to her dorm room to discuss the program. When he discovered that Alycia was alone, he raped her.

In the painful aftermath, Alycia grappled with depression and reached out to her closest college friend. "Before, we were inseparable," Alycia told us. "But when she found out about the rape, she said, 'I can't talk to you.'" Alycia sought support from other friends and got similar responses. One of them even admitted, "I know this has been really hard for you, but it has also been really hard for *me*." The friend was feeling guilty for failing to stop the assault and was personalizing the tragedy. Alycia reassured her that she wasn't to blame, but the friend stopped talking to Alycia, choosing escape over empathy.

"The assault was obviously shocking for me," Alycia said. "When I decided to report it, there was a lot of tension. It was a pretty affluent community, mainly rich and mainly white. Being black, I felt intimidated. But just as shocking was the response of my friends. I felt helpless." Luckily, her friends from high school stepped up, and she was able to transfer to a different college and move into an apartment with new roommates who helped her recover. Alycia shared her story on the Lean In community website in the hopes of encouraging other rape survivors to speak out. She wrote that she was determined to pursue her original goals—and she succeeded, graduating from college and getting a job she loves in Middle Eastern affairs and security.

For friends who turn away in times of difficulty, putting distance between themselves and emotional pain feels like self-preservation. These are the people who see someone drowning in sorrow and then worry, perhaps subconsciously, that they will be dragged under too. Others get overwhelmed by a sense of helplessness; they feel there's nothing they can say or do to make things better, so they choose to say and do nothing. But what we learn from the stress experiment is that the button didn't need to stop the noise to relieve the pressure. Simply showing up for a friend can make a huge difference.

I was lucky to be surrounded by loved ones who not only showed up but often figured out what I needed before I knew myself. For the first month, my mom stayed to help me take care of my son and daughter . . . and take care of me. At the end of each endless day, my mom lay down next to me and held me until I cried myself to sleep. I never asked her to do it; she just did. The day she left, my sister Michelle took her place. For the next four months, Michelle came over multiple nights each week, and when she couldn't, she made sure a friend filled in.

Needing that much help was awful for me, but just entering the bedroom that I used to share with Dave made me feel like someone had knocked the wind out of me. Bedtime became the symbol of all that had changed. The grief and anxiety built throughout the day to that moment when I knew I'd have to crawl—and I mean crawl—into bed alone. By showing up night after night, and making it clear that they would always be there when I needed them, my family and friends were my button.

My closest friends and family convinced me that they truly wanted to help, which made me feel like less of a burden. Every time I told Michelle to go home, she insisted that she wouldn't be able to rest unless she knew I was asleep. My brother David called me from Houston every single day for more than six months. When I thanked him, he said that he was doing it for himself because the only time he felt okay was when he was talking to me. I learned that at times, caring means that when someone is hurting, you cannot imagine being anywhere else.

This constant support was vital for me but might not be for everyone. A woman who also lost her husband shared that at first she dreaded being alone at night. Her mother stayed with her for two weeks and then she went to her brother's. She deeply appreciated all the help but admitted, "After a month, I was *so* ready to just be alone."

It's hard to understand—or even imagine—another person's pain. When we're not in a physically or emotionally intense state, we underestimate its impact. In one experiment, people were asked to put their arm in a bucket of water and guess how painful it would be to sit in a freezing room for five hours. When the bucket was filled with ice water, they predicted that sitting in the room would be 14 percent more painful than when the bucket was filled with warm water. But when people made their predictions just ten minutes after removing their arm from the ice water, they made the same estimates as the warm water group. Once the icy water was behind them, even for just minutes, they couldn't quite fathom what it felt like to be cold. (On the bright side, there are very few situations in real life where you find yourself with your arm in a bucket of ice water.)

There's no one way to grieve and there's no one way to comfort. What helps one person won't help another, and even what helps one day might not help the next. Growing up, I was taught to follow the Golden Rule: treat others as you want to be treated. But when someone is suffering, instead of following the Golden Rule, we need to follow the Platinum Rule: treat others as *they* want to be treated. Take a cue from the person in distress and respond with understanding—or better yet, action.

As I was struggling to get back on my feet at home and at work, friends and colleagues would graciously ask, "Is there anything I can do?" They were sincere, but for most of them, I did not have an answer. There were things that would have been helpful but it was hard for me to ask for them. And some of the requests that came to mind were way too much of an imposition. *Can you make sure my children and I are never left alone on any holiday?* Or impossible. *Can you invent a time machine so we can go back and say good-bye to Dave—or at least skip Father's Day?*

Author Bruce Feiler believes the problem lies in the offer to "do anything." He writes that "while well meaning, this gesture unintentionally shifts the obligation to the aggrieved. Instead of offering 'anything,' just do something." Bruce points to friends who sent packing supplies to someone who was moving out after getting divorced and others who held a "fire shower," a variation on a bridal shower, for a friend who had lost her home. My colleague Dan Levy told me that when his son got sick and he was by his side at the hospital, a friend texted him, "What do you NOT want on a burger?" Dan appreciated the effort. "Instead of asking if I wanted food, he made the choice for me but gave me the dignity of feeling in control." Another friend texted Dan that she was available for a hug if he needed one and would be in the hospital lobby for the next hour whether he came downstairs or not.

Specific acts help because instead of trying to fix the problem, they address the damage caused by the problem. "Some things in life cannot be fixed. They can only be carried," therapist Megan Devine observes. Even the small act of holding someone's hand can be helpful. Psychologists put teenage girls under stress by asking them to give a spontaneous public speech. When mothers and daughters who were close held hands, the physical contact took away some of the daughters' anxiety. The daughters sweated less and the physiological stress was transferred to the mothers.

This effect resonates with me. Four days after I found Dave on the gym floor, I gave a eulogy at his funeral. I initially thought I would not be able to get through it, but my children wanted to say something and I felt that I had to show them I could too. My sister Michelle stood beside me and gripped my hand tightly. I didn't know about the mother-daughter study then, but her hand in mine gave me courage.

Dave was a constant source of strength—a button not just for me but for so many. Now where would his friends and family turn for support? A helpful insight comes from psychologist Susan Silk, who devised the "ring theory." She suggests writing down the names of people in the center of the tragedy and drawing a circle around them. Then draw a bigger circle around that one and write the names of the people who are next most affected by the event. Keep drawing larger circles for people based on proximity to the crisis. As Silk writes with mediator Barry Goldman, "When you are done you have a Kvetching Order."

Adam drew the first four circles of my ring like this:

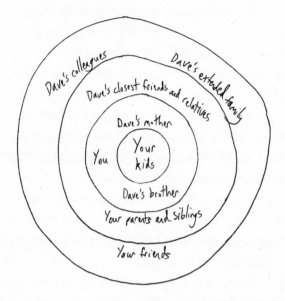

Wherever you are in the circle, offer comfort in and seek comfort out. That means consoling the people who are closer to the tragedy than you are and reaching out for support from those who are farther removed.

Sometimes I sought support from those in the outer rings, but other times I was afraid to accept it. About a week after the funeral, I went to my son's flag football game still in that deep, early fog that makes it hard to imagine that there even is such a thing as a children's football game. Looking around for a place to sit, I saw so many fathers watching their sons. *Dave will never be at another football game again.* Just as I was lowering the baseball hat on my head to hide my tears, I spotted my friends Katie and Scott Mitic waving me over to a blanket they had laid out on the grass. Earlier, they had offered to attend the game with me, but because they have their own kids to take care of, I told them not to come. I was so grateful they hadn't listened. They sat on either side of me, holding my hands. I was there for my son . . . and they were there for me.

Of course, some people just want to curl up after tragedy and hide in their ring. A friend in Los Angeles was utterly lost after her only son died in a car accident. When friends would invite her over to dinner, her initial impulse was always to say no even though she'd been social in the past. They would press and she would force herself to say yes. Then the day before she'd want to cancel but would remind herself, "This is just you trying to run away. You have to go."

I was torn by similar conflicting emotions. I hated asking for help, hated needing it, worried incessantly that I was a huge burden to everyone, and yet depended on their constant support. I was suffering from so many insecurities that I almost started a People Afraid of Inconveniencing Others support group, until I realized that all the members would be afraid of imposing on one another and no one would show up.

Before, I defined friendships by what I could offer: career advice, emotional support, suggestions for old (and Dave would have added bad) TV shows to watch. But this all changed and I needed so much help. I did not just feel like a burden . . . I truly was a burden. I learned that friendship isn't only what you can give, it's what you're able to receive.

Still, as everyone I know who has been through tragedy acknowledges with sadness, there are friends who don't come through as you might hope. A common experience is having friends who decide it's their job to inform grieving pals what they should be doing—and worse, what they should be feeling. A woman I met chose to go to work the day after her husband died because she could not bear to be at home. To this day, she still feels the disapproval of colleagues who said to her, "I'd think you'd be too upset to be here today." *You would think, but you just don't know.*

Grief doesn't share its schedule with anyone; we all grieve differently and in our own time. "It's been three months. When are you gonna get over this?" one woman said to a friend who miscarried. After the one-year mark, a friend commented to me, "You should be done with that grief thing." *Really? Okay, I'll just put that inconvenient "grief thing" into a drawer.* It's also probably not the most helpful thing to tell someone who's grieving, "You're so depressed and angry. It's just too hard to be around you." That one was said right to my face and preyed upon my worst fear—that it was true.

Anger is one of the five stages of grief famously defined by psychiatrist Elisabeth Kübler-Ross. In the face of loss, we're supposed to start in denial and move to anger, then to bargaining and depression. Only after we pass through these four stages can we find acceptance. But now experts realize that these are not five stages. They are five states that don't progress in a linear fashion but rise and fall. Grief and anger aren't extinguished like flames doused with water. They can flicker away one moment and burn hot the next.

I struggled with anger. A friend might say the wrong thing and I would react way too strongly, sometimes lashing out— "That is just not helpful"—or bursting into tears. Sometimes I caught myself and apologized right away. But other times I did not realize what I'd done until later or, I imagine, at all. Being my friend meant not just comforting me in my grief but dealing with a level of anger that I'd never felt before and struggled to control. My anger scared me—and made me need the comfort of my friends even more. Like the people in the stress experiment who were consoled by the simple presence of a button, I needed friends who let me know that even if I was difficult to be around, they would not abandon me.

Lots of people nicely tried to assure me, "You will get through this," but it was hard to believe them. What helped me more was when people said that they were in it with me. Phil Deutch did this time and again, saying, "*We* are going to get through this." When he was away, he sent emails, sometimes with just one line: "You are not alone." One of my childhood girlfriends sent a card that read, "One day she woke up and understood we are all in this together." That card has hung above my desk ever since.

I started spending more time with my closest friends and family, who taught me by example how to live the Platinum Rule. At first, it was survival; I could be myself with them, and they were able to absorb and help carry the anguish and anger. Later, it became my choice. These shifts in relationships happen to most of us naturally over time. As people mature, they focus on a smaller set of meaningful relationships, and the quality of friendships becomes a more important factor in happiness than the quantity.

As the worst of the grief faded, I had to restore balance in my friendships so they weren't one-sided. About a year after Dave died, a friend seemed distracted and upset. I asked what was going on and she hesitated to tell me. I pressed and she admitted that she and her husband weren't getting along, but she knew that if she compared her situation to mine, she shouldn't complain. I joked that if my friends couldn't complain about their partners, I wouldn't have any friends. I wanted those close to me to know I was there to help carry their troubles too.

As time passed, I felt especially grateful to my family and friends who continued to check in and show up. On the six-month anniversary of Dave's death, I sent them a poem, "Footprints in the Sand." It was originally a religious parable, but to me it also expressed something profound about friendship. The poem relates a dream of walking on the beach with God. The storyteller observes that in the sand there are two sets of footprints except during those periods of life filled with "anguish, sorrow or defeat." Then there is only one set of footprints. Feeling forsaken, the storyteller challenges God: "Why, when I needed you most, have you not been there for me?" The Lord replies, "The years when you have seen only one set of footprints, my child, are when I carried you."

I used to think there was one set of footprints because my friends were carrying me through the worst days of my life. But now it means something else to me. When I saw one set of footprints, it was because they were following directly behind me, ready to catch me if I fell.

4

Self-Compassion and
Self-Confidence

Coming to Grips with Ourselves

WHEN CATHERINE HOKE WAS twenty-five years old, she and her husband went on a church trip to Romania to help care for orphans living with HIV. She returned home to New York committed to doing more for those in need. Then a friend invited her to join a Christian outreach visit to a Texas prison. At the time, Catherine was working in venture capital and noticed that many of the inmates had the same skills and drive as great entrepreneurs. She started flying to Texas on weekends to teach business classes at the prison. She learned that nearly one in four Americans has a criminal history and one in twenty will serve time. While most are eager to work after release, their criminal records make it difficult to get jobs. Catherine felt strongly that these men deserved a second chance.

Catherine quit her job and invested all of her savings to create the nonprofit Prison Entrepreneurship Program, which prepares formerly incarcerated men to find employment and start their own businesses. Within five years, the program expanded into a statewide organization that graduated six hundred students and launched sixty start-ups. The governor of Texas honored Catherine's work with a public service award.

Then Catherine's personal life fell apart. After nine years of marriage, her husband asked for a divorce unexpectedly and left without saying good-bye. "This was the darkest period of my life," Catherine told us. "In my community, divorce was often seen as a sin. People said, 'God hates divorce.'" She was afraid to talk about her situation. But there was one group she knew wouldn't judge her: the graduates of her program. Knowing they had felt the sharp sting of prejudice, she turned to them for support. They helped her move out of her house and became her closest confidants. During this emotional time, she lost sight of boundaries and ended up having intimate relationships with more than one of the graduates. The men had been released from prison, so Catherine hadn't broken any laws, but the Texas Department of Criminal Justice determined that her behavior was inappropriate. Catherine was banned from Texas prisons and informed that her program would be banned too if she stayed involved. She resigned and her departure made national headlines as a "prison sex scandal."

Catherine had spent years urging employers and donors to be open-minded, asking them to imagine how they'd feel if they were defined by their biggest mistake. Suddenly that was her own life. "I violated my spiritual values. I felt like I was covered in the thickest wall of shame," she told us. "I lost my identity as a leader. I was dead broke financially. I didn't want to live anymore because I felt like I had ruined God's calling for my life." She attempted suicide.

Catherine had dedicated herself to helping people get a second chance. She had fostered compassion for ex-offenders. Now she needed to find compassion for someone else—herself.

Self-compassion isn't talked about as much as it should be,

maybe because it's often confused with its troublesome cousins, self-pity and self-indulgence. Psychologist Kristin Neff
describes self-compassion as offering the same kindness to ourselves that we would give to a friend. It allows us to respond to
our own errors with concern and understanding rather than
criticism and shame.

Everyone makes mistakes. Some are small but can have
serious consequences. We turn our heads for a split second on
the playground at just the moment our child falls. We change
lanes and hit the car in our blind spot. We make big mistakes
too—errors of judgment, failures to follow through on commitments, lapses of integrity. None of us can change what we
have already done.

Self-compassion comes from recognizing that our imper-
fections are part of being human. Those who can tap into it
recover from hardship faster. In a study of people whose marriages fell apart, resilience was not related to their self-esteem,
optimism, or depression before divorce, or to how long their
relationships or separations had lasted. What helped people
cope with distress and move on was self-compassion. For soldiers returning from war in Afghanistan and Iraq, those who
were kind to themselves showed significant declines in symptoms of post-traumatic stress disorder (PTSD). Self-compassion
is associated with greater happiness and satisfaction, fewer
emotional difficulties, and less anxiety. Both women and men
can benefit from self-compassion, but since women tend to be
harder on themselves, they often benefit more. As psychologist
Mark Leary observes, self-compassion "can be an antidote to
the cruelty we sometimes inflict on ourselves."

Self-compassion often coexists with remorse. It does not
mean shirking responsibility for our past. It's about making
sure that we don't beat ourselves up so badly that we damage

our future. It helps us realize that doing a bad thing does not necessarily make us a bad person. Instead of thinking "if only I weren't," we can think "if only I hadn't." This is why confession in the Catholic religion begins with "Forgive me, Father, for I have sinned," not "Forgive me, Father, for I am a sinner."

Blaming our actions rather than our character allows us to feel guilt instead of shame. Humorist Erma Bombeck joked that guilt was "the gift that keeps giving." Although it can be hard to shake, guilt keeps us striving to improve. People become motivated to repair the wrongs of their past and make better choices in the future.

Shame has the opposite effect: it makes people feel small and worthless, leading them to attack in anger or shrink away in self-pity. Among college students, the shame-prone were more likely than the guilt-prone to have drug and alcohol problems. Prisoners who felt ashamed were 30 percent more likely to commit repeat offenses than those who felt guilty. Elementary and middle school kids who felt shame were more hostile and aggressive, while guilt-prone kids were more likely to defuse conflicts.

Bryan Stevenson, a legal activist who leads the Equal Justice Initiative, makes the point that "we are all broken by something. We have all hurt someone." He deeply believes that "each of us is more than the worst thing we've ever done." This is what Catherine Hoke came to understand. The first person she sought out was her pastor, who encouraged her to forgive herself and make amends. "The way for me to have compassion for myself was to own my mistakes," she told us. She wrote a frank and remorseful letter to all 7,500 volunteers and supporters of her program admitting what she'd done. More than a thousand responses poured in from people who thanked Catherine for her honesty and said they believed in her. Many asked what she was doing next. Even though she couldn't see a future for herself, others could. "It was those people who loved me back to life," she recalls. She started to feel self-compassion.

Writing to others—and to herself—turned out to be key to Catherine's ability to rebound. For as long as she can remember, Catherine has kept a journal. "Journaling isn't exactly meditating," she told us. "But it helped me quiet myself and reflect. I was able to put words to my feelings and unpack them."

Writing can be a powerful tool for learning self-compassion. In one experiment, people were asked to recall a failure or humiliation that had made them feel bad about themselves, ranging from flunking a big test to flopping in an athletic competition to forgetting lines in a play. They drafted a letter to themselves expressing the understanding they would offer to a friend in the same situation. Compared to a control group who wrote just about their positive attributes, those who were kind to themselves were 40 percent happier and 24 percent less angry.

Turning feelings into words can help us process and overcome adversity. Decades ago, health psychologist Jamie Pennebaker had two groups of college students journal for fifteen minutes a day for just four days—some about nonemotional topics and others about the most traumatic experiences of their lives, which included rape, attempted suicide, and child abuse. After the first day of writing, the second group was less happy and had higher blood pressure. This made sense, since confronting trauma is painful. But when Pennebaker followed up six months later, the effects reversed and those who wrote about their traumas were significantly better off emotionally and physically.

Since then, more than a hundred experiments have documented the therapeutic effect of journaling. It has helped medical students, patients with chronic pain, crime victims, maximum-security prisoners, and women after childbirth. It has crossed cultures and countries from Belgium to Mexico to New Zealand. Writing about traumatic events can decrease anxiety and anger, boost grades, reduce absences from work, and lessen the emotional impact of job loss. Health benefits include higher T-cell counts, better liver function, and stronger antibody responses. Even journaling for a few minutes a few times can make a difference. "You don't have to write for the rest of your life," Pennebaker told us. "You can start and stop when you feel you need to."

Labeling negative emotions makes them easier to deal with. The more specific the label, the better. "I'm feeling lonely" helps us process more than the vague "I'm feeling awful." By putting feelings into words, we give ourselves more power over them. In one study, people with a phobia of spiders learned they were going to interact with one. But first the participants were instructed to distract themselves, think of the spider as nonthreatening, do nothing, or label their feelings about the spider. When the spider showed up, those who labeled their fear exhibited significantly less physiological arousal and were more willing to approach it.

There are some caveats. Immediately after a tragedy or crisis, journaling can backfire: the event is too raw for some to process. After loss, it appears that writing can reduce loneliness and improve mood but does not necessarily help with grief or depression symptoms. Still, for many, constructing a story can lead to insight. For those who don't enjoy writing, talking into a voice recorder works just as well. There seems to be less benefit to expressing trauma without language through art, music, or dance (but at least there'll be no hurt feelings if your angry abstract painting falls into the wrong hands).

Journaling helped Catherine identify thoughts that were holding her back, like "People will only love me when I have something to offer them" and "Relying on other people makes me weak and needy." Psychologists call these "self-limiting beliefs," and Catherine decided to replace them with what she calls "self-freeing" beliefs. She wrote, "My worth isn't tied to my actions" and "I can allow other people to care for me—and I need to take care of myself."

After a year of therapy, Catherine was ready to renew her commitment to helping people defy the odds and defy their pasts. Starting fresh in New York, she launched Defy Ventures, a program that provides current and former inmates with mentoring and training to start businesses. In one of the courses she created, students learn how to pinpoint their own self-limiting beliefs and rewrite them as self-freeing beliefs. This year, I had a chance to visit a prison with Catherine. I saw her help the inmates, Entrepreneurs-in-Training as she calls them, define themselves by their future goals instead of their past traumas and mistakes. Six years in, Catherine reports that Defy Ventures has aided more than 1,700 graduates and incubated and funded 160 start-ups, achieving a 95 percent employment rate with just 3 percent recidivism.

Catherine regained her self-confidence not only professionally but in her personal life too. In 2013, she married Charles Hoke, who believed so strongly in the Defy mission that a year after their wedding he left his job in finance to work with her. "I have my second chance as a wife. I have my second chance at life," Catherine said. "I have my second chance to extend second chances to others."

Self-confidence is critical to happiness and success. When we lack it, we dwell on our flaws. We fail to embrace new challenges and learn new skills. We hesitate to take even a small risk that can lead to a big opportunity. We decide not to apply for a new job, and the promotion we miss becomes the moment our career stalled. We don't muster the courage to ask for a first date, and the future love of our life becomes the one who got away.

Like many, I've struggled with self-doubt throughout my life. In college, every time I took an exam, I feared that I'd failed. And every time I didn't embarrass myself or even did well, I believed that I'd fooled my professors. I later learned that this phenomenon is called the impostor syndrome, and while both women and men feel it, women tend to experience it more intensely. Nearly two decades later, after seeing this same self-doubt hold back so many women at work, I gave a TED talk that encouraged women to "sit at the table." This talk became the basis for my book *Lean In*. Researching and being open about how I'd grappled with insecurity helped me understand ways to build my self-confidence. As I urged other women to believe in themselves and act on what they would do if they weren't afraid, I learned these lessons myself.

Then I lost Dave. When a loved one dies, we expect to be sad. We expect to be angry. What we don't see coming—or at least I didn't—is that trauma can also lead to self-doubt in *all* aspects of our lives. This loss of confidence is another symptom of pervasiveness: we are struggling in one area and suddenly we stop believing in our capabilities in other areas. Primary loss triggers secondary losses. For me, my confidence crumbled overnight. It reminded me of watching a house in my neighborhood that had taken years to build get torn down in a matter of minutes. Boom. Flattened.

My first day back in the office after Dave's death, Mark and I were in a meeting with the Facebook ads team. To illustrate a point, I turned to Boz, our head of product and engineering, and said, "You remember this from when we worked on it together at Google." It would have been a fine thing to say . . . except that Boz never worked with me at Google. He started his career at Google's then rival Microsoft.

In the next meeting, I wanted to make sure I contributed something. *Anything.* Someone directed a question at a colleague but I jumped in to answer . . . and went on and on. Somewhere in the middle, I realized I was rambling, but I kept going, unable to stop. Later that night, I called Mark to say that I knew I'd made a total fool of myself. Twice. *That I remembered.* "Don't worry," Mark said. "Thinking Boz worked at Google is the kind of mistake you would've made before." *Very comforting.*

Actually, it *was* comforting. But even if I had made those kinds of mistakes before, now it was all I could focus on. Then Mark pointed out a few things I'd said in the meetings that he thought were on target—none of which I remembered. He went on to say that neither he nor anyone else expected me to be able to hold it together all the time. This comment helped me set more reasonable expectations and stop being so hard on myself. Mark's compassion started me down the path of learning to have compassion for myself. I felt deep gratitude for having such a supportive boss, and I know not everyone does. Many jobs don't even allow employees time off to grieve or care for their families. Compassion at work shouldn't be a luxury; it's important to develop policies that give people the time off and support they need so we don't have to rely on the kindness of our bosses.

Bolstered by Mark and a pep talk from my father that night, I returned to work the next day. And the next day. And the days after that. But on so many of those days, my grief prevented me from thinking clearly. In the middle of a meeting, an image of Dave's body on that gym floor would flash before my eyes. It was like augmented reality—I knew that I was in a Facebook conference room, but it felt like his body was there too. Even when I was not seeing his image, I was crying constantly. Lean in? I could barely stand up.

Journaling became a key part of my recovery. I began on the morning of Dave's funeral, four days after he died. "Today I will bury my husband" was the first line I wrote. "This is the unthinkable. I have no idea why I want to write all of this down—as if I could forget any detail."

I had been trying to keep a journal since childhood. Every couple of years I would start a new one, only to give up just a few days later. But over the five months following Dave's funeral, 106,338 words poured out of me. I felt like I couldn't breathe until I wrote everything down—from the smallest detail of my morning to the unanswerable questions of existence. If I went even a few days without journaling, the emotions would build up inside me until I felt like a dam about to burst. At the time, I didn't understand why writing on an inanimate computer was so important. Shouldn't I be talking to my family and friends, who could actually respond? Wouldn't it be better to try to distance myself from the anger and grief rather than use the limited time I had alone each day to dredge it all up?

Now it's clear that my compulsion to write was guiding me in the right direction. Journaling helped me process my overwhelming feelings and my all-too-many regrets. I thought constantly about how if I'd known that Dave and I had only eleven years, I would've made sure we spent more time together. I wished that in the hard moments in our marriage, we had fought less and understood each other more. I wished that on what turned out to be our last anniversary, I had stayed home rather than flying with my kids to attend a bar mitzvah. And I wished that when we went for a hike that final morning in Mexico, I'd walked by Dave's side and held his hand, instead of walking with Marne while he walked with Phil. As I wrote out these moments, my anger and regret began to lessen.

Philosopher Søren Kierkegaard said that life can only be understood backward but it must be lived forward. Journaling helped me make sense of the past and rebuild my self-confidence to navigate the present and future. Then Adam suggested that I should also write down three things that I'd done well each day. At first, I was skeptical. I was barely functioning; what moments of success could I find? *Got dressed today. Trophy please!* But there is evidence that these lists help by focusing us on what psychologists call "small wins." In one experiment, people wrote down three things that went well and why every day for a week. Over the next six months, they became happier than a group writing about early memories. In a more recent study, people spent five to ten minutes a day writing about things that went "really well" and why; within three weeks, their stress levels dropped, as did their mental and physical health complaints.

For six months, almost every night before I went to bed, I made my list. Since even the most basic tasks were hard, I started with those. *Made tea. Got through all of my emails. Went to work and focused for most of one meeting.* None of these were heroic accomplishments, but that little notebook by my bed served an important purpose. It made me realize that for my entire life I'd gone to bed thinking about what I'd done wrong that day, how I'd messed up, what wasn't working. Just the act of reminding myself of anything that had gone well was a welcome shift.

Making gratitude lists has helped me in the past, but this list served a different purpose. Adam and his colleague Jane Dutton found that counting our blessings doesn't boost our confidence or our effort, but counting our contributions can. Adam and Jane believe that this is because gratitude is passive: it makes us feel thankful for what we receive. Contributions are active: they build our confidence by reminding us that we can make a difference. I now encourage my friends and colleagues to write about what they have done well. The people who try it all come back with the same response: they wish they'd started doing this sooner.

Slowly, I began to regain my self-confidence at work. I told myself the things I've told others who doubted themselves: I didn't have to aim for perfection. I didn't have to believe in myself all the time. I just had to believe I could contribute a little bit and then a little bit more. I'd experienced this phenomenon of incremental progress when I went skiing for the first time at age sixteen. To say that I am not a natural athlete is a serious understatement. On my fourth day on skis, my mother and I took a wrong turn and wound up on a difficult run. I looked down the mountain, panicked, and fell into the snow, knowing it would be impossible for me to get down alive. My mom told me not to look at the bottom but instead just take ten turns. She coaxed me to get up and then helped me count ten turns out loud. After those ten turns, I did another ten. Then another. Eventually, I found my way to the bottom. Over the years, this lesson has stuck with me whenever I feel overwhelmed. *What would you do if you weren't afraid?* I'd take one turn. Then another.

As people saw me stumble at work, some of them tried to help by reducing pressure. When I messed up or was unable to contribute, they waved it off, saying, "How could you keep anything straight with all you're going through?" In the past, I had said similar things to colleagues who were struggling, but when people said it to me, I discovered that this expression of sympathy actually diminished my self-confidence even more. What helped was hearing, "Really? I thought you made a good point in that meeting and helped us make a better decision." *Bless you.* Empathy was nice but encouragement was better.

Self-doubt sneaks up even on those who see it coming. Adam's friend and fellow psychologist Jenessa Shapiro was diagnosed with metastatic breast cancer in her thirties. Her primary fear was dying, but her secondary fear was losing her job. While working on a paper, Jenessa had trouble writing and immediately started wondering, "Are chemo and cancer destroying my ability to think?" As her productivity fell, she worried that she would be denied tenure and end up unemployed. She was also concerned about how others would view her. As an expert on stigma, she suspected that her cancer would make people doubt her capabilities. Jenessa joined several colleagues to test this hypothesis, and sure enough, cancer survivors were less likely to get called back for job interviews. When she wasn't invited to give a presentation, she wondered, "Do people know I'm sick and don't want to bother me? Or do they think I'm not up to the challenge?"

Jenessa's husband helped her look at her situation with more self-compassion, reminding her, "When you didn't have cancer, you couldn't write a paper in a day." Her coworkers helped as well. As Jenessa told us, "On the whole people treat me like I am capable—someone who can still make valuable contributions. Of course, it is also stressful if people expect me to do everything that I did before, so I imagine it must be a difficult balancing act for my colleagues to hit the sweet spot between expecting too little and too much of me." Jenessa's story and my experience have changed the way I interact with coworkers going through difficult personal situations. I still always start by offering them time off. But now I understand the importance of treating them as regular members of the team and praising their work as well.

Jenessa was thankful when she received tenure, but the fear of joblessness is widespread. In 2015, there were nearly 45 million people unemployed in India and nearly 24 million in the European Union; in South Africa, a million and a half people had been unemployed for more than five years. Anyone who's ever been fired, downsized, or forced to leave a job knows how devastating it can be. Not only does loss of income put people under tremendous financial pressure, it can also bring about secondary losses by triggering depression, anxiety, and other health problems. Losing a job is a blow to self-esteem and self-worth and can rip away identities. By robbing people of a sense of control, losing income can actually lower their ability to tolerate physical pain. And the stress can spill over into personal relationships, resulting in increased conflict and tensions at home.

To help people suffering from depression after job loss, psychologists at the University of Michigan held weeklong workshops at churches, schools, libraries, and city halls. For four hours each morning, hundreds of unemployed people attended a program designed to build their job search confidence. They identified marketable skills and sources of job leads. They rehearsed interviews. They made a list of setbacks they might face and strategies for maintaining motivation. They found small wins. In the next two months, people who had participated in this program had a 20 percent greater chance of landing a new job. And for the next two years, they were more confident and more likely to stay employed. To be clear, no one is suggesting that self-confidence is a cure for unemployment; we need to provide education and support so people can find jobs and social insurance benefits to help them when they can't. But programs like this can make a difference.

Self-confidence at work is important and often discussed, but self-confidence at home is just as crucial and often overlooked. Being a single parent was uncharted territory for me. Dave and I had always discussed even the smallest decisions concerning our children; I thought many times about how the night Dave died I had not even wanted to make a decision on my own about my son's ripped sneakers. Suddenly, our decade-long conversation about parenting came to an abrupt stop.

When I wrote *Lean In*, some people argued that I did not

spend enough time writing about the difficulties women face when they don't have a partner. They were right. *I didn't get it.* I didn't get how hard it is to succeed at work when you are overwhelmed at home. I wrote a chapter titled "Make Your Partner a Real Partner" about the importance of couples splitting child care and housework 50/50. Now I see how insensitive and unhelpful this was to so many single moms who live with 100/0. My understanding and expectation of what a family looks like has shifted closer to reality. Since the early 1970s, the number of single mothers in the United States has nearly doubled. Worldwide, 15 percent of children are in single parent households and women head approximately 85 percent of these households.

I will never experience or fully understand the challenges many single moms face. Although the odds are stacked against them, they do everything they can to raise incredible children. To try to make ends meet, many have more than one job—not including the job of being a mother. And high-quality child care is often prohibitively expensive. The costs of placing a four-year-old and an infant in child care exceed annual median rent payments *in every U.S. state.*

Despite their hard work, single mothers have higher rates of poverty than single fathers in most countries, including the U.K., Australia, South Africa, and the U.S.—where almost a third of single mothers and their children experience food insecurity, and families headed by black and Latina single mothers face even more challenges, with poverty rates approaching 40 percent. While we advocate for policy changes to support these families, we also need to do all we can to offer more immediate help. Shockingly, one in three families in the San Francisco Bay Area needs food assistance. I started volunteering years ago at my local food bank, Second Harvest, then helped launch the Stand Up for Kids campaign, which now provides meals to almost 90,000 kids every month. After the campaign began distributing food at a local charter school, student disciplinary problems decreased. "People thought we had bad kids," the principal told us, "but we had hungry kids." Another school reported that the program reduced student absenteeism and health complaints and increased academic performance.

Working moms, especially those who are single, are put at a disadvantage from the start. The United States is the only developed country in the world that does not provide paid maternity leave. In Australia, maternity leave is paid at the federal minimum wage; in India, less than one percent of working women are eligible for maternity benefits. And many women and men don't have access to the sick and bereavement leave they need to get through difficult times—which makes it more likely that personal struggles will lead to work struggles. Adam's research has shown that this is shortsighted: offering support through personal hardships helps employees become more committed to their companies. We need to rethink our public and corporate policies to make sure that women and men get the time off they need to care for themselves and their families.

We also need to banish the outdated assumption that children live with two married heterosexual parents. Once Dave died, the world kept reminding me and my children of what we no longer had. From father-daughter dances to Portfolio Night at school, father-child events were *everywhere*. My brother David said that he too realized for the first time how many father events there were at their public school in Houston and how hard that must be for the many children without dads.

Judgment calls loomed before me, making me feel increasingly incapable. *What would Dave have done?* Day after day I wished I knew and wished even more that he were here to answer the questions himself. But just like at work, when I focused on small steps, it was easier. I saw that I didn't have to know how to help my kids with every situation they would encounter. I didn't have to help them with what they were facing right then. I did not have to take even ten turns. I just had to help them take one turn at a time.

I started by making a few decisions . . . then immediately questioned those decisions. Anything that seemed to violate Dave's preferences, no matter how small, rattled me. Dave believed that sleep was critically important for our children and adamantly opposed sleepovers. But after he passed away, I found that sleepovers comforted and distracted my kids. I knew this change was inconsequential, but it seemed symbolic to me of how hard it was to live without Dave and still honor his wishes. My sister-in-law Amy pointed out that Dave never got to tell me how his views would have evolved in the face of devastating loss. I could then picture him saying, "Yes, of course, if it makes them happier, they can have sleepovers." And while I'll never know what Dave would think about small decisions like whether preteens can watch *Pretty Little Liars* or if it's okay for them to play Pokémon GO, I do know what he wanted for our kids more than a good night's sleep. Integrity. Curiosity. Kindness. Love.

Without Dave as a rudder, I found myself relying heavily on feedback from friends and family. Like when colleagues pointed to something positive at work, it helped when friends let me know they thought I'd handled something well at home. It also helped when they were honest about how I could do things better, like suggesting I be more flexible with previous rules and more patient with both my children and myself.

As I got farther from the trauma and the newness of life without Dave, I found myself journaling less. I no longer felt like I was going to burst without this outlet. The day after what would have been Dave's forty-eighth birthday, I decided I had to try to move on from this phase of my mourning. I sat down and wrote this:

October 3, 2015

This is the last entry of this journal. The longest 22½ weeks—
156 days—I have ever lived. I am pushing myself to move onward
and upward—and part of that is to stop writing this journal.
I think I am ready.

I dreaded yesterday since the day Dave died. I knew it would
be a marker—the birthday that did not happen. Anytime anyone
said it would be Dave's birthday, I corrected them in my mind
and sometimes out loud. No, it will not be his birthday. You have
to be alive to have a birthday. He is not. October 2, 2015, was the
day he would have turned 48. 48 years old. Half a life.

Went to his grave with Paula, Rob, Mom, Dad, David, and
Michelle. It looked so much smaller than it loomed in my memory
from the day we buried him.

Towards the end of our time there, I sat down in front of the
grave by myself. I spoke to him out loud. I told him that I loved
him and that I missed him every minute of every day. I told him
how empty the world seemed without him in it. And then I just
cried, as it was so painfully clear that he could not hear me.

David and Michelle gave me a few minutes alone and then
came over and sat down next to me, one on each side. Something
so comforting about this—I realized that my siblings were in my
life long before Dave was. We talked about how if we were lucky,
the three of us would live long enough to bury our parents—and
we would do it there—together. And so life continues with them.
Not with Dave but with them. I can grow old with David and
Michelle by my side as they always have been.

Looking at Dave's grave, I realized that there is nothing left to
do or say. I don't get to tell him I love him ever again. I don't get
to hold him or kiss him ever again. I have learned how to make
sure I talk about him constantly so our children remember him
but I will never again have another conversation with him about

them. I can cry all day every day—but it will not bring him back. Nothing will.

We are all headed for where Dave is. Without a doubt. Looking at the row upon row of headstones, it is so clear that we all end up in the ground. So each day has to count. I don't know how many I have left and I want to start living again.

I am not happy yet. But I know how much I have done these past five months. I know I can survive. I know I can raise my kids. I know I need a ton of help—and have learned to ask for it—and I believe more and more that the core people are in this with me for the long haul. It is still scary but less so. As all of them tell me over and over, I am not alone. We all need other people—and I do more than ever. But at the end of the day the only person who can move my life ahead, make me happy, and build a new life for my kids is me.

156 days in. Hopefully many more to go. So today I end this journal. And try to restart the rest of my life . . .

5

Bouncing Forward

The One I Become Will Catch Me

In the depths of winter, I finally learned that within me
there lay an invincible summer.

—ALBERT CAMUS

S A PHYSICIAN, Joe Kasper devoted most of his career to treating patients with life-threatening illnesses. Still, when his teenage son Ryan was diagnosed with a rare and fatal form of epilepsy, he felt completely at a loss. "In a few short moments, I learned my son's fate and there was nothing I could do about it—no hope for a cure," Joe wrote. "It was like seeing my son tied to a railroad track with a locomotive right around the bend and having to look on in helpless frustration and despair."

A traumatic experience is a seismic event that shakes our belief in a just world, robbing us of the sense that life is controllable, predictable, and meaningful. Yet Joe was determined not to get sucked into the void. "When we are no longer able to change a situation," psychiatrist and Holocaust survivor Viktor Frankl observed, "we are challenged to change ourselves."

After his son's diagnosis, Joe wanted to learn everything he could about recovery from trauma. His search led him to the work of UNC Charlotte professors Richard Tedeschi and Lawrence Calhoun. The two psychologists were treating grieving parents and expected to see signs of devastation and post-traumatic stress, which they did. But they also found something surprising. The parents were all suffering and would have done anything to bring their children back. At the same time, many also described some positive outcomes in their lives following loss. It seems hard to believe, but as time passed, instead of post-traumatic stress, some of the parents experienced post-traumatic *growth*.

Psychologists went on to study hundreds of people who had endured all kinds of trauma: victims of sexual assault and abuse, refugees and prisoners of war, and survivors of accidents, natural disasters, severe injuries, and illnesses. Many of these people experienced ongoing anxiety and depression. Still, along with these negative emotions there were some positive changes. Up to that point, psychologists had focused mostly on two possible outcomes of trauma. Some people struggled: they developed PTSD, faced debilitating depression and anxiety, or had difficulty functioning. Others were resilient: they bounced back to their state before the trauma. Now there was a third possibility: people who suffered could bounce *forward*.

Adam told me about post-traumatic growth four months after Dave died. It didn't sound real to me. Too catchphrasey. Too unlikely. Sure, there might be people who could grow from tragedy, so you could hold this out as hope to someone who had just lost her husband. But it wasn't going to happen for me.

Adam understood my skepticism and admitted that he didn't

even mention this possibility for the first few months because he knew I would dismiss it. But now he thought I was ready. He told me that more than half the people who experience a traumatic event report at least one positive change, compared to the less than 15 percent who develop PTSD. Then he did something super annoying: he quoted me to me. "You often argue that people can't be what they can't see," Adam said. "That girls aren't studying computer science because they don't see women in computer science. That women don't reach for leadership roles because they don't see enough women in leadership roles. This is the same thing. If you don't see that growth is possible, you're not going to find it." I agreed I would try to see it. And I had to admit that post-traumatic growth sounded a lot better than a life filled with sadness and anger.

That's when I learned about Joe Kasper. Tragically, his son Ryan died three years after the diagnosis, thrusting Joe into what he describes as "the emotional tsunami of his death. If there is anything more painful in life, I hope never to discover it." Joe vowed not to let the tsunami pull him under. He decided to study positive psychology at the University of Pennsylvania, where Adam was one of his professors. Joe learned that post-traumatic growth could take five different forms: finding personal strength, gaining appreciation, forming deeper relationships, discovering more meaning in life, and seeing new possibilities. But Joe wanted to do more than study Tedeschi and Calhoun's findings; he wanted to live them.

Nietzsche famously described personal strength as "what does not kill me makes me stronger." Tedeschi and Calhoun have a slightly softer (one could say less Nietzschean) take: "I am more vulnerable than I thought, but much stronger than I ever imagined." When we face the slings and arrows of life, we are wounded and the scars stay with us. But we can walk away with greater internal resolve.

I can't imagine. People continued to say this to me and I agreed with them. It was all I could do to live through the moments when it hurt so much. In the depths of acute grief, I did not think I would be capable of growing stronger. But as excruciating days turned into weeks and then months, I realized that I *could* imagine because I was living it. I had gained strength just by surviving. In the words of an old adage: "Let me fall if I must fall. The one I become will catch me."

Slowly, very slowly, a new sense of perspective began seeping into my daily life. In the past, when my children faced challenges I would get anxious and Dave would reassure me. Now it is up to me to stay calm on my own. Before, if my daughter came home upset that she didn't make the soccer team with her friends, I would've encouraged her to keep practicing while secretly worrying that she was disappointed. Now I think, "This is great. A normal kid problem! What a relief to be in a normal-problem zone." *Note to self: think these thoughts but do not say them out loud.*

My childhood friend Brooke Pallot endured an arduous adoption process filled with huge disappointments, which melted away when she finally held her baby. In the happy months that followed, Brooke met Meredith, another new mom. Meredith had struggled to get pregnant and the two women bonded over their "miracle babies." The kids connected too, becoming what Brooke called "little baby besties." Then one day Meredith found a small lump under her armpit. She was only thirty-four and felt perfectly healthy but had it checked anyway. A PET scan revealed that she had stage 4 breast cancer. In addition to offering Meredith her full support, Brooke felt compelled to get her own mammogram. When she tried to schedule it, her gynecologist's office advised her to wait half a year until she turned forty and insurance would cover the cost. But Brooke insisted on the test, which revealed that she had stage 4 breast cancer too.

The two friends went through chemotherapy together. Brooke responded to the treatment, but Meredith's cancer had already spread to her liver. She died three years later. "I always tell her parents, her husband, and her daughter that she was my angel," Brooke now says. "What saved me is that they caught my cancer before it had gone to any vital organs. And that is because of Meredith."

Brooke has been in remission for seven years and in addition to gaining physical strength, she has gained emotional strength. "I went through chemo and buried my young friend. That gives you perspective whether you're looking for it or not. The little things don't stress me out. I am much stronger, much more centered and reasonable now. Something that sent me spinning before I now see as relative to what could have been and I am like, 'Ah, that's nothing. I am here.'"

This is the second area of post-traumatic growth that Tedeschi and Calhoun identified: gaining appreciation. In the first month after Dave died, I received an amazingly supportive call from Kevin Krim. Kevin and I had only met in passing, but we had close friends in common and I knew he had suffered an unthinkable tragedy. In 2012, after a swimming lesson with their three-year-old daughter Nessie, Kevin's wife Marina returned to their New York apartment to find that their nanny had stabbed their six-year-old daughter Lulu and their two-year-old son Leo to death.

When I saw Kevin months after his loss, I could barely speak, not knowing what if anything to say. Now he was calling to comfort me. I asked Kevin how in the world he had gotten through it. He told me that in his eulogy he explained, "I worry that we might be tempted, in the face of such obliterating darkness, to retreat from the world, but . . . I heard this quote that I think is very important here. It goes, 'He who has a why to live for can bear almost any how.' Marina and Nessie, you are my WHY." Kevin told me how grateful he felt that his daughter had survived and his marriage was strong. He and Marina decided to have more children and they felt fortunate that they were able to. Since Lulu and Leo loved art, Kevin and Marina started ChooseCreativity.Org, a nonprofit that teaches creativity to disadvantaged children. Kevin and Marina are finding post-traumatic growth by adding more love and beauty to the world . . . which is an act of love and beauty itself.

It is the irony of all ironies to experience tragedy and come out of it feeling more grateful. Since I lost Dave, I have at my fingertips this unbelievable reservoir of sadness. It's right next to me where I can touch it—part of my daily life. But alongside that sadness, I have a much deeper appreciation for what I used to take for granted: family, friends, and simply being alive. My mom offered a helpful comparison. For sixty-six years, she never thought twice about walking, but as she aged, her hip deteriorated and walking became painful. After hip replacement surgery four years ago, she feels grateful for every step she is able to take without pain. What she feels on a physical level, I feel on an emotional level. On the days that I'm okay, I now appreciate that I'm walking without pain.

There were times when I'd felt this appreciation before. After college, I worked for the World Bank's India health team on leprosy eradication. I visited treatment centers and hospitals all over India and met hundreds of patients, many of whom had been kicked out of their villages and were living in abject poverty and isolation. My first trip lasted a month. I got through each day trying to be professional and then cried myself to sleep each night. It put all of my problems into perspective. I remember thinking that I would never complain about anything in my life again—I would appreciate my good fortune to be born into a community with the resources to invest in health care. But over the years, that perspective faded and life went back to how it was before.

Now I'm determined to hold on to this gratitude. When I asked Brooke how she does it, she said she reminds herself regularly of what she could have lost. "I'm watching Meredith's daughter grow up and trying to be present in her life in every way that I can. Each time I look at my little girl, I remember that my friend isn't here to raise her daughter. I know how lucky I am." Brooke makes a conscious effort to mark the milestones. "Every year I celebrate that I got another year with my daughter," Brooke told me. "Seven years ago I didn't think I would see her second birthday."

After loss, the emptiness of birthdays, anniversaries, and holidays can be especially hard. Brooke encouraged me to see these milestones as moments to be cherished. I used to celebrate my birthday every five years, feeling like only the birthdays with the zeros and fives were special occasions. Now I celebrate every one because I no longer take for granted that the next birthday will come. Long gone are the jokes I used to make about not wanting to grow old (and working for a boss who is fifteen years my junior, I used to make those jokes *a lot*). After we lost Dave, my friend Katie Mitic started writing letters to her friends on their birthdays, letting them know how much they mean to her. Some of her friends have followed her lead, showing pre-traumatic growth. They learned lessons in life that I learned only from death.

Last fall, Malala Yousafzai and her father Ziauddin came to my house to discuss her work fighting for all girls to have access to education. They stayed for dinner with Katie, her husband Scott, and my kids, and we all went around the table to share our best, worst, and grateful moments of the day. Scott said that he had spent the past week worried about how one of their children was adjusting to a new school, but listening to Malala reminded him how grateful he should be that his kids have a school to attend. Malala then shared her own gratitude story. She told us that after she was shot by the Taliban, her mother started giving her birthday cards dated from the beginning of her recovery. When Malala turned nineteen, the card said, "Happy 4th birthday." Her mother was reminding her daughter—and herself—that Malala was lucky to be alive.

We don't have to wait for special occasions to feel and show gratitude. In one of my favorite studies, people were asked to write and deliver a thank-you note to someone who had shown them unusual kindness. This pleased the receivers but it also made the note writers feel significantly less depressed, and the gratitude afterglow stayed with them for a month. When Adam shared this research with me, I realized why it works: in the moments I spend thanking my friends and family, my sadness is pushed into the background.

My friend Steven Levitt lost his one-year-old son Andrew to meningitis in 1999. Sixteen years later, he told me that "with each passing year, the balance tipped a little more toward an appreciation of what there once was and away from the horror of what was lost." As time has passed, I too have greater appreciation for the time Dave and I spent together and for the time I have now.

Eleven days before the anniversary of his death, I broke down crying to a friend. We were sitting—of all places—on a bathroom floor. I said, "Eleven days. One year ago, he had eleven days left. And he had no idea." Looking at each other through tears, we asked how he would have lived if he had known he had only eleven days left—and if we could live going forward with the understanding of how precious every single day is.

Tragedy does not always leave us appreciating the people in our lives. Trauma can make us wary of others and have lasting negative effects on our ability to form relationships. Many survivors of sexual abuse and assault report that their beliefs about the goodness of others remain shattered and they have difficulty trusting people. After losing a child, parents often have a harder time getting along with relatives and neighbors. After losing a spouse, it's common for people to argue more with friends and feel insulted by them.

But tragedy can also motivate people to develop new and deeper relationships. This is the third area of post-traumatic growth. Soldiers who experience significant losses during war are more likely to have friendships from their service forty years later. After heavy combat, they value life more and prefer to spend their time with people who share that understanding. Many breast cancer survivors report feeling greater intimacy with family and friends.

When people endure tragedies together or endure the same tragedy, it can fortify the bonds between them. They learn to trust each other, be vulnerable with each other, depend on each other. As the saying goes: "In prosperity our friends know us. In adversity we know our friends."

One of the most striking examples of how adversity can drive people to build stronger connections is Stephen Thompson. Growing up, he and his four younger siblings were frequently homeless, sleeping in shelters and cars. His mother struggled with severe drug and alcohol problems and the family often went hungry, sometimes stealing food from local grocery stores. Stephen had to take care of his siblings and missed so much school that he fell behind. His teachers assumed he had learning disabilities and placed him in special education classes. Once, while he was living with his grandmother, a SWAT team came looking for his mom, who hid behind a door. A police-

man later explained that she and her boyfriend had blown up a
bridge during a political protest.

When Stephen was nine years old, his mother abandoned
him and his siblings in a hotel room. It took three days before
child protective services found them. This turned out to be the
bottom that Stephen was able to kick against to start his rise
to the surface. "Our lives before were unbearably stressful,"
he said. "When she left us in that hotel, it was almost a gift—
a new beginning for us."

Stephen believes that his resilience came from learning at
a young age to view this extreme trauma as a chance to form
new relationships. He spent a few months in a foster home on a
street near his siblings and was then sent to live in a state home
for children. Once he started going to school regularly, he was
able to form stable friendships. His new friends invited him
over for Thanksgiving and Christmas and he had the chance to
celebrate the holidays with their families. Then the mother of a
close friend changed everything by asking Stephen to live with
them permanently. "It was one of the most powerful lessons
of my life, because it really showed me the kindness of others," Stephen told us. "I realized that friends can become your
family." He made a pact with himself to always be there for his
friends. "To call at tough times. To really try and connect with
people and get to know them." I got to know Stephen when we
worked together at Google, where he turned his remarkable
ability for connecting with people into a career as an executive
recruiter.

The fourth form of post-traumatic growth is finding greater
meaning in life—a stronger sense of purpose rooted in a belief
that one's existence has significance. In Viktor Frankl's words,
"In some way, suffering ceases to be suffering at the moment it
finds a meaning."

Many find meaning in discovering religion or embracing

spirituality. Traumatic experiences can lead to deeper faith, and people with strong religious and spiritual beliefs show greater resilience and post-traumatic growth. Rabbi Jay Moses, who officiated at my and Dave's wedding, told me that "finding God or a higher power reminds us that we are not the center of the universe. There is much we don't understand about human existence, and there is order and purpose to it anyway. It helps us feel that our suffering is not random or meaningless."

Yet that suffering can also test our faith in God's benevolence. Laverne Williams, a church deacon from Montclair, New Jersey, told us that when she was struggling with depression and her sister was diagnosed with cancer, she questioned God. "There are times when I've been angry at God—'How can you let this happen?'" she said. But then she remembered that "it's not about praying to God to fix everything. He's not a magic genie where you can ask for certain things and only the good things pop out." Still, her faith helped her reject permanence: "Even when you are in the darkest hours you can stay hopeful. That's the thing about faith . . . it helps you know that sooner or later this too shall pass."

Last spring, I read an open letter from NFL veteran Vernon Turner to his younger self. The letter graphically described how he was conceived: his mother was an eighteen-year-old track star who was attacked on the street, injected with heroin, and gang-raped. When Vernon was eleven years old, he walked in on his mother shooting heroin in their bathroom. Instead of sending him out, she said, "I want you to see me do this because I don't ever want you to do this. . . . Because this is going to kill me." Four years later, her words proved tragically true. At first, a stepfather took care of Vernon and his four younger siblings, but during Vernon's freshman year of college, his stepfather passed away too. Not even twenty years old, Vernon was solely responsible for his family.

I was so moved by the letter that I reached out to him. Vernon explained to me that at that point, he hit rock bottom. "I thought I was being punished. First God took my mom, then my dad. Now I was going to lose my family. I got on my knees and prayed. I asked God to show me how to help my family." Vernon thought the only way he could earn enough money to provide for them was to play in the NFL. He was a star for a Division II college team but had been told repeatedly that he wasn't tall enough, strong enough, or talented enough to turn pro. "I had to make it, because if I didn't my brothers and sisters would be in foster care. I was not going to be a product of my DNA. I was going to be a product of my actions," he wrote.

Vernon was driven by a clear purpose. He began setting his alarm for two a.m. to start his workouts, building strength by tying a rope around his body and dragging a tire up a hill. "I pushed myself to the limit mentally and physically. I put myself through brutal hell preparing for the NFL. I had workouts I would not wish on my worst enemy—I was ready to die on the football field." He made it into the league as a return specialist. "What triggered resilience for me," he said, "was God giving me strength and my mom telling me, right before she died, that no matter what happens, you keep the family together. I turned to football to save my family. When they measured my stature, they failed to measure my heart."

Family and religion are the greatest sources of meaning for many people. But work can be another source of purpose. The jobs where people find the most meaning are often ones that serve others. The roles of clergy, nurses, firefighters, addiction counselors, and kindergarten teachers can be stressful, but we rely on these often undercompensated professionals for health and safety, learning and growth. Adam has published five different studies demonstrating that meaningful work buffers against burnout. In companies, nonprofits, government, and the military, he finds that the more people believe their jobs help others, the less emotionally exhausted they feel at work and the less depressed they feel in life. And on days when people think they've had a meaningful impact on others at work, they feel more energized at home and more capable of dealing with difficult situations.

After Dave's death, my work became more meaningful to me; I connected with the Facebook mission of helping people share in a way that I never had before. In 2009, my friend Kim Jabal's brother died by suicide on his fortieth birthday. Suffering from shock, her family didn't think they could handle a memorial service. But "people wanted to share their stories, to support us, and to support each other," Kim told me at the time. "They did it on Facebook. An outpouring of love and support came through—every day we would read more stories, see more photos, learn about someone else who knew him and loved him."

The same thing happened for me. I did not truly understand how important Facebook could be to those suffering from loss until I experienced it myself. During his eulogy for Dave, our friend Zander Lurie was describing Dave's generosity when he stopped midsentence and did something that none of us had ever seen before at a funeral: he asked everyone to "raise your hand if Dave Goldberg did something to change your life for the better—provided a key insight, a valuable connection, help when you were down." I looked behind me and saw hundreds of arms shooting into the air. There was no way to hear all those stories that day, and even if I had, I was in no state to remember them. But many are now preserved on Dave's Facebook profile. Person after person, some with names I'd never heard, shared how Dave took time to help them get a job, start a business, support a cause. Our friend Steve Fieler posted a video of Dave cheering at a baseball game and wrote, "Dave reminded me how good it feels to cheer . . . and to be cheered for. He made me feel in the moment. In Silicon Valley where 'what's next' trumps 'what's now,' it's rare to be as warm and present as Dave."

For those who have the opportunity, pursuing meaningful work can help with recovery from trauma. When my friend Jeff Huber lost his wife to colon cancer, I passed along what many had told me: don't make any big decisions in the early stages of acute grief. Fortunately, Jeff ignored my advice. He quit his job to become CEO of GRAIL, a company that aims to detect cancer in its earliest phases. "It's like you've been through a portal," Jeff told me. "You can't go back. You're going to change. The only question is how." Like Joe Kasper, who could not save his son Ryan, Jeff knows he couldn't save the one he loved most, but he hopes that earlier cancer detection will save millions of lives within the next decade. He says that he now gets out of bed every morning faster and with more energy than he ever has in his life.

Jeff has found meaning through the fifth kind of post-traumatic growth—seeing new possibilities. Tedeschi and Calhoun found that after trauma, some people ended up choosing different directions for their lives that they never would have considered before. In the wake of the terrorist attacks of September 11, some Americans made dramatic changes in their careers. They joined fire departments, enlisted in the military, and entered the medical professions. Applications to Teach for America tripled, and many of the aspiring teachers said their interest stemmed from 9/11. Those seeking a change wanted to use their precious time to contribute to something larger than themselves. Before the attacks, work might have been a job; afterward, some wanted a calling. People were also more likely to find meaning after surviving a tornado, a mass shooting, or a plane crash if they believed they were going to die during the event. After being reminded of their mortality, survivors often re-examine their priorities, which in some cases results in growth. A brush with death can lead to a new life.

It's not an easy pivot. Trauma often makes it harder to pursue new possibilities. Caring for loved ones who are sick can mean that family members have to work less or stop working altogether; almost three million Americans are caring for an adult with cancer, which takes an average of thirty-three hours a week. Along with the loss of income, high medical costs frequently decimate family budgets. Illness is a factor in more than 40 percent of bankruptcies in the U.S., and there's evidence that people with cancer are more than 2.5 times more likely to file for bankruptcy. Even relatively small unexpected expenses can have disastrous consequences: 46 percent of Americans are unable to pay an emergency bill of four hundred dollars. For people living on the edge, paid family leave, quality health care, and mental health coverage can make the difference between hanging on and falling off.

Tragedy does more than rip away our present; it also tears apart our hopes for our future. Accidents shatter people's dreams of being able to support their families. Severe illnesses prevent people from finding work or love. Divorce erases future anniversaries (although I have a friend who celebrates her breakup each year). These profound shifts in self-perception are another secondary loss and a risk factor for depression. Our possible selves—who we hoped to become—can be collateral damage.

Although it can be extremely difficult to grasp, the disappearance of one possible self can free us to imagine a new possible self. After tragedy, we sometimes miss these opportunities because we spend all of our emotional energy wishing for our old lives. As Helen Keller put it, "When one door of happiness closes, another opens; but often we look so long at the closed door that we do not see the one which has been opened for us."

For Joe Kasper, the breakthrough occurred when he realized that his actions could be part of his son's legacy. While studying for his master's degree, Joe created a therapeutic process called "co-destiny," which encourages bereaved parents to view their child's life in a larger framework so that death does not become the end of the story. Parents who seek purpose and meaning from their tragedies can go on to do good, which then becomes part of their child's impact on the world. As Joe explained, "I realized that my destiny was to live my life in a way that would make my son proud. The awareness that I could add goodness to my son's life by doing good in his name motivates me to this day."

It's not surprising that so many trauma survivors end up helping others overcome the adversity that they have faced themselves. "There is nothing more gratifying than helping someone else escape this quagmire of despair," Joe told us. "I know this passion of mine is an area of personal growth related to my trauma. Helping others grow from their traumas reflects back to my son's life." After undergoing a hardship, people have new knowledge to offer those who go through similar experiences. It is a unique source of meaning because it does not just give our lives purpose—it gives our *suffering* purpose. People help where they've been hurt so that their wounds are not in vain.

While we are grieving, it can be hard to see through the pain to new possibilities or greater meaning. When my mom left to go home after staying with me for the first month, I was terrified. As she hugged me good-bye, she told me about a conversation she'd had with Scott Pearson, a family friend. "The week Dave died, Scott said, 'This is the end of one chapter and the beginning of the next.' I didn't tell you then because I didn't think you would've believed him. But I have believed it all along . . . and so should you." I am not sure I could have heard this a month earlier, but on that day it gave me hope. To quote the Roman philosopher Seneca (and the song "Closing Time"): "Every new beginning comes from some other beginning's end."

A few years ago, Dave and I took our children to see the play *Wicked*. On the way out, one of us shouted enthusiastically, "That's my favorite musical!" You might guess it was our preteen daughter, but it wasn't. It was Dave. His favorite song was "For Good," when the two lead characters say good-bye and acknowledge that they may never see each other again. Together, they sing:

> *I do believe I have been changed for the better.*
> *And because I knew you . . .*
> *I have been changed*
> *For good.*

Dave will always be, as the song says, "a handprint on my heart." He changed me in profound ways by his presence. And he changed me in profound ways by his absence.

It's my deepest desire that something good will come from the horror of Dave's death. When people say they have found comfort or strength in what I've shared, it honors the life Dave lived. He did so much to help others, and I hope this book reaches people and becomes part of his legacy. Perhaps this is our co-destiny.

6

Taking Back Joy

THE FIRST WEEK of middle school, my best friend informed me that I wasn't cool enough to hang out with. This hurtful breakup turned out to be a blessing. Soon after I was dumped, three girls picked me up. We became friends for life, adding three more to our circle in high school. Mindy, Eve, Jami, Elise, Pam, and Beth—or as we still call ourselves, "the Girls." The Girls have advised me on everything from what to wear to prom to what job to take to what to do when a baby wakes up at midnight . . . and again at three a.m.

In the fall of 2015, Beth's daughter was becoming a bat mitzvah. Part of me didn't want to go. Just days before he died, Dave and I had picked a date for our son's bar mitzvah. The thought that Dave would not be at our child's ceremonial transition to adulthood cast a giant pall over the occasion. But during the dark days of that summer, the Girls had checked in daily and took turns coming to California. By showing up again and again, they proved to me that I was not alone. I wanted to be there for them in the happy times, just as they'd been there for me in the sad.

Sitting with the Girls and their families at the bat mitzvah service felt deeply comforting, almost as if I had been trans-ported back to when we were teenagers, to the innocent days when a bad haircut was a big problem. Beth's daughter crushed the Torah reading and we all teared up with pride. The cer-emony ended with the traditional reciting of the Kaddish, the prayer for those who have died. Instantly, six hands reached out to me from in front, in back, and across the pew. My friends held me tightly and, as they had promised, we got through it together.

At the party that night, our kids ran around having a great time. I watched my son and daughter chatting away with their "almost cousins" and thought there should be a word for the joy you feel when your kids are friends with your friends' kids. In addition to the Girls, there were other guests from our Miami school days, including the cutest boy in our class: Brook Rose. Even his name is perfect. Back then, none of us believed we had a chance with him, and after college he confirmed that when he told us he's gay.

The DJ started playing "September" by Earth, Wind & Fire and Brook reached for my hand. "Come on," he said, flashing his gorgeous smile. He led me to the dance floor, and just like in high school we let go, dancing and singing. And then I burst into tears.

Brook quickly maneuvered me to the outdoor patio and asked what was wrong. At first, I assumed I was missing Dave, except I knew *exactly* what that felt like and somehow this was different. Then it dawned on me. Dancing to an upbeat song from childhood had taken me to a place where I wasn't filled with loneliness and longing. I wasn't just feeling okay. I actually felt *happy*. And that happiness was followed immediately by a flood of guilt. How could I be happy when Dave was gone?

The next day, my kids and I headed to Philadelphia to visit Adam and his family. I told Adam about my meltdown on the dance floor. He wasn't surprised. "Of course this was the first moment you were happy," he told me. "You haven't been doing a single thing that brings you joy."

Adam was right. For more than four months, I'd been completely focused on my kids, my job, and just making it through each day. I had stopped doing anything Dave and I had done together for fun like seeing movies, going out to dinner with friends, watching *Game of Thrones,* or playing Settlers of Catan or Scrabble. Catan was especially upsetting to me since we'd been playing during our last moments together.

There were plenty of reasons to hole up. I didn't want to leave my kids with a babysitter even after they fell asleep in case they woke up. I was afraid that if I tried to go out, I'd end up crying in public, embarrassing myself and ruining everyone else's good time. I had made one attempt to be social early that fall. I invited a small group of friends over to watch a movie. We started the evening with frozen yogurt in the kitchen, and I kept thinking, *You can do this. Pretend everything's normal.* The movie had been recommended by a friend as fun and light. We started watching. So far so good. Then a few minutes in, the main character's wife died. I thought the froyo was going to come back up. Everything was not normal.

In my Facebook post thirty days into widowhood, I wrote that I'd never have another moment of pure joy. When friends who had lost spouses assured me that this wasn't true and someday I would feel happy again, I doubted them. Then Earth, Wind & Fire proved me wrong. But the moment of happiness on the dance floor was fleeting, barely rearing its head before guilt whacked it back into its hole.

Survivor guilt is a thief of joy—yet another secondary loss from death. When people lose a loved one, they are not just wracked with grief but also with remorse. It's another personalization trap: "Why am I the one who is still alive?" Even after acute grief is gone, the guilt remains. "I didn't spend enough time with him." And death isn't the only kind of loss that triggers guilt. When a company lays off employees, those who keep their jobs often struggle with survivor guilt. The thought process begins with "It should've been me." This is followed by gratitude—"I'm glad it wasn't me"—which is quickly washed away by shame: "I'm a bad person for feeling happy when my friends lost their jobs."

A life chasing pleasure without meaning is an aimless existence. Yet a meaningful life without joy is a depressing one. Until that moment on the dance floor, I did not realize I'd been holding myself back from happiness. And even that fleeting moment was ruined by guilt, making my prediction that I'd never feel pure joy again seem accurate. Then one day on the phone Dave's brother Rob gave me a true gift. "Since the day Dave met you, all he ever wanted was to make you happy," Rob told me, his voice choking up. "He would want you to be happy—even now. Don't take that away from him." My sister-in-law Amy helped too by making me see how much my mood affected my children. They had told her they were feeling better because "Mommy stopped crying all the time."

When we focus on others, we find motivation that is difficult to marshal for ourselves alone. In 2015, U.S. Army major Lisa Jaster was attempting to graduate from the elite Ranger School. Having served in Afghanistan and Iraq, she thought she could complete the grueling program in nine weeks. But getting through land navigation, water survival, staged assaults, ambushes, mountaineering, and an obstacle course took her twenty-six weeks. The final event was a twelve-mile march carrying a thirty-five-pound rucksack plus nine quarts of water and a rifle. By the ten-mile mark, Lisa felt nauseous, her feet were blistered, and she thought there was no way she could make it to the finish line. But then an image flashed through her mind—a cherished picture of her and her kids. Her son had Batman on his T-shirt and her daughter had Wonder Woman on hers. On the photo Lisa had written, "I want to be their superhero." Lisa ran the last two miles and beat her target time by a minute and a half. She went on to make history as one of the first three women to become an Army Ranger. When I met Lisa, I told her she wasn't just her kids' superhero. I shared her story at the dinner table and now she's a hero to my kids too.

With Rob's and Amy's words ringing in my ears, I decided to try having fun for my children—and *with* my children. Dave had loved playing Catan with our kids because it taught them to think ahead and anticipate opponents' moves. One afternoon, I took the game down from the shelf. I asked my kids matter-of-factly if they wanted to play. They did. In the past, I was always orange. My daughter was blue. My son was red. Dave was gray. When just the three of us sat down to play, my daughter pulled out the gray pieces. My son got upset and tried to take them away from her, insisting, "That was Daddy's color. You can't be gray!" I held his hand and said, "She can be gray. We take things back."

"We take it back" became our mantra. Rather than give up the things that reminded us of Dave, we embraced them and made them an ongoing part of our lives. We took back rooting for the teams that Dave loved: the Minnesota Vikings and the Golden State Warriors. We took back poker, which Dave had played with our kids since they were young. They laughed at the story about how one day Dave came home from work to find them playing poker *at ages five and seven* and said it was one of the proudest moments of his life. Chamath Palihapitiya, our friend who had played poker with Dave frequently and enthusiastically, stepped in to continue their Texas Hold'em education. I would have tried but I don't think Dave would have wanted them to learn from a "lousy player"—Dave's words, but boy did Chamath agree *frequently and enthusiastically*.

For myself, I took back *Game of Thrones*. It wasn't nearly as much fun as watching with Dave, who had read the entire series of books and could track who was plotting against whom. But I focused, caught up, and ended the season rooting for Khaleesi and her dragons, just as Dave and I would have together. I started having friends over to watch movies, looking more carefully for ones where no one loses a spouse. And my best take-back was finding the perfect online Scrabble opponent. Dave and I had played together. Dave and Rob had played together. Now Rob and I play each other. I am a poor substitute since the two brothers were evenly matched; in almost a hundred games, I've beaten Rob a grand total of once. But now for just a few minutes on our phones throughout the day, Rob and I are connected to each other . . . and to Dave.

We want others to be happy. Allowing ourselves to be happy—accepting that it is okay to push through the guilt and seek joy—is a triumph over permanence. Having fun is a form of self-compassion; just as we need to be kind to ourselves when we make mistakes, we also need to be kind to ourselves by enjoying life when we can. Tragedy breaks down your door and takes you prisoner. To escape takes effort and energy. Seeking joy after facing adversity is taking back what was stolen from you. As U2 lead singer Bono has said, "Joy is the ultimate act of defiance."

One of the comments on my thirty-day Facebook post that affected me most deeply was from a woman named Virginia Schimpf Nacy. Virginia was happily married when her husband died suddenly in his sleep at age fifty-three. Six and a half years later, the night before her daughter's wedding, Virginia's son died of a heroin overdose. She insisted on going forward with the wedding and planned her son's funeral the next day. Soon, Virginia was working with her local school district on a drug prevention program, joining forces with parents and counselors to create a grief support group, and advocating for legislative changes to fight addiction. She also looked for ways to counter her sadness. She started watching old Carol Burnett shows and went on a cross-country road trip with her chocolate Labrador to visit her daughter and son-in-law. "Both deaths are woven into the fabric of my life, but they're not what define me," she said. "Joy is very important to me. And I can't count on joy to come from my daughter or anyone else. It has to come from me. It is time to kick the shit out of Option C."

When we look for joy, we often focus on the big moments. Graduating from school. Having a child. Getting a job. Being reunited with family. But happiness is the frequency of positive experiences, not the intensity. In a twelve-year study of bereaved spouses in Australia, 26 percent managed to find joy after loss as often as they had before. What set them apart was that they re-engaged in everyday activities and interactions.

"How we spend our days," author Annie Dillard writes, is "how we spend our lives." Rather than waiting until we're happy to enjoy the small things, we should go and do the small things that make us happy. After a depressing divorce, a friend of mine made a list of things she enjoyed—listening to musicals, seeing her nieces and nephews, looking at art books, eating flan—and made a vow to do one thing on the list after work each day. As blogger Tim Urban describes it, happiness is the joy you find on hundreds of forgettable Wednesdays.

My New Year's resolution for 2016 was based on this idea. Each night, I was still trying to write down three things I had done well, but as my confidence returned, this seemed less necessary. Then Adam suggested a new idea: write down three moments of joy every day. Of all the New Year's resolutions

I've ever made, this is the one I've kept the longest by far. Now nearly every night before I go to sleep, I jot down three happy moments in my notebook. Doing this makes me notice and appreciate these flashes of joy; when something positive happens, I think, *This will make the notebook*. It's a habit that brightens the whole day.

Many years ago, a mentor of mine, Larry Brilliant, tried to teach me that happiness requires work. Larry and I had grown close while starting Google's philanthropic initiative, so I was heartbroken when his son Jon was diagnosed with lung cancer at age twenty-four. Jon was treated at Stanford and often spent nights at our house since we lived closer to the hospital. He brought his treasured childhood Lego sets to play with my kids, and to this day, when my kids play with Legos I think of Jon.

For a few months, it looked like Jon had made a miraculous recovery, so when he died a year and a half later, his family was doubly shattered. Larry's deep spirituality helped build his resilience. For ten years, Larry and his wife Girija had lived in India, where they studied with a Hindu guru and practiced Buddhist meditation. After losing their son, they focused their spiritual work on turning some of the pain into gratitude for the years when Jon was healthy. At Dave's funeral, Larry sobbed with me, saying that he never expected us to be grieving for another loved one so soon. Then, with his hands on my shoulders, as if to hold me up, he said he'd be there to make sure the pain didn't drown me. "A day of joy is fifteen minutes. A day of pain is fifteen years," he said. "No one pretends this is easy, but the job of life is to make those fifteen minutes into fifteen years and those fifteen years into fifteen minutes."

Paying attention to moments of joy takes effort because we are wired to focus on the negatives more than the positives. Bad events tend to have a stronger effect on us than good events.

This made sense in prehistoric times: if you weren't haunted by the memory of the time someone you loved ate the poisonous berries, you might nibble on them yourself. But today we give that attention to ordinary setbacks and daily hassles. A broken windshield wiper or a coffee stain has the power to drag us down. We zero in on potential threats and miss opportunities to smile.

Just as labeling negative emotions can help us process them, labeling positive emotions works too. Writing about joyful experiences for just three days can improve people's moods and decrease their visits to health centers a full three months later. We can savor the smallest of daily events—how good a warm breeze feels or how delicious French fries taste (especially when snatched from someone else's plate). My mom is one of the most optimistic people I know, and when she gets in bed each night she always spends a few moments being grateful for the comfort of the pillow under her head.

As we get older, we define happiness less in terms of excitement and more in terms of peacefulness. Reverend Veronica Goines sums this up as, "Peace is joy at rest, and joy is peace on its feet." Sharing positive events with another person also increases our own pleasant emotions over the next few days. In the words of Shannon Sedgwick Davis, a human rights advocate whose work requires her to deal with atrocities on a daily basis, "Joy is a discipline."

A friend of mine who lost his wife of forty-eight years right after his seventieth birthday told me that to fight despair he needed to shake up his routine. Doing the same things he'd done with his wife left him yearning for his old life, so he made a concerted effort to seek out new activities. He advised me to do the same. Along with taking things back, I looked for ways to move forward. I started small. My kids and I began playing hearts, a card game my grandfather taught me (and one I'm better at than poker). We began biking on weekends, which Dave couldn't do because it hurt his back. I started playing the piano again, something I hadn't done in thirty years. I play badly due to a lack of talent compounded by a lack of practice. Still, plinking out a song makes me feel better. "It gives me a smile," to paraphrase a Billy Joel song I play badly and sing off-key, "to forget about life for a while."

Playing music at the edge of our capabilities is what psychologists call a "just manageable difficulty." This level requires all of our attention, giving us no room to think about anything else. Many of us remember being happiest in flow—the state of total absorption in a task. When you're in a deep conversation with a friend and suddenly realize that two hours have flown by. When you take a road trip and the dashed line becomes a rhythm. When you're engrossed in reading a Harry Potter book and forget Hogwarts isn't real. *Total Muggle mistake.* But there's a catch. Mihaly Csikszentmihalyi, who pioneered this research, found that people don't report being happy while they are in flow. They are so engaged that they only describe it as joyful afterward. Even trying to survey people about their flow states jolted them right out of it. *Good work, psychologists.*

Many turn to exercise for flow. After losing his wife, comedian Patton Oswalt noticed that comic books like Batman portrayed strange reactions to grief. In real life, "if Bruce Wayne watched his parents murdered at 9, he wouldn't become this buff hero," Oswalt said. "How about someone dies, and they just get fat and angry and confused? But no, immediately, they're at the gym." Actually, hitting the gym—or just the pavement for a brisk walk—can be hugely beneficial. The physical health effects of exercise are well known, including lower risk of heart disease, high blood pressure, stroke, diabetes, and arthritis. Many doctors and therapists also point to exercise as one of the best ways to improve psychological well-being. For some adults over fifty who suffer from major depression, working out may even be as effective as taking an antidepressant.

Flow might sound like a luxury, but after tragedy it can become essential. Four years ago in Syria, Wafaa (last name not included to protect her family's security) fell into despair when her husband was arrested. He has not been seen or heard from since. Just a few months before that, her sixteen-year-old son was killed while playing soccer outside their apartment. Wafaa couldn't bear the pain and considered taking her own life, but she was pregnant with her sixth child and that stopped her. She and her brother fled to Istanbul with her two youngest children, while her three older children stayed behind in Syria. Not long after, she received a call from her daughter, who had a son of her own. He had just been killed by a sniper a week before his second birthday. Beyond unimaginable. Unfathomable.

Wafaa's experience is horrifyingly common. There are more refugees today than there have been at any time since World War II; more than 65 million people have had their lives viciously torn apart. If Option B for me means coping with the loss of a spouse, Option B for refugees means coping with loss upon loss upon loss: loss of loved ones, home, country, and all that is familiar. When I read Wafaa's story, I was struck by her incredible resilience and got in touch to learn more. She opened up about her struggles. "When my son was murdered, I thought I would die," she told us through a translator. "Being a mother saved me. I need to smile for my other children."

When Wafaa arrived in Turkey, she spent most days alone with her children while her brother tried to find work. She did not speak the language, knew almost no one, and felt overwhelmingly lonely. Then she found a community center for Syrians and met other women who were also struggling. Little by little, Wafaa found moments of joy. "Praying makes me happy," she said. "My relationship with God is stronger. I understand him more and I know he will keep giving me strength."

Along with prayer, she finds comfort and flow in making meals for her family and friends. "Some days, time moves slowly and I think too much. Cooking gives me something to look forward to. Cooking is like breathing in Syria. It gives me oxygen. I'm not a painter, but I love creating. The smells . . . the feel of the meat. No matter where I am, I can try to re-create home. Cooking gives me comfort and helps me focus. Sometimes I lose myself in the cooking. Then the time goes quickly. My mind goes quiet." When one of Wafaa's neighbors in Istanbul became sick, Wafaa made her food every day for a week. "It filled me with happiness to think I could help her with food—and Syrian food! It was my way to say, 'Take this from my homeland. I have nothing else to give.'" Caring for her children and others is a source of joy for Wafaa. As she told us, "When my children smile, I feel happiness. I feel that I'm still here for a reason. I will be healed through healing them."

Whether you see joy as a discipline, an act of defiance, a luxury, or a necessity, it is something everyone deserves. Joy allows us to go on living and loving and being there for others.

Even when we're in great distress, joy can still be found in moments we seize and moments we create. Cooking. Dancing. Hiking. Praying. Driving. Singing Billy Joel songs off-key. All of these can provide relief from pain. And when these moments add up, we find that they give us more than happiness; they also give us strength.

7

Raising Resilient Kids

THIS EXQUISITELY DETAILED PAINTING of two children from South Carolina is by award-winning painter Timothy Chambers. Tim has been a professional artist for more than thirty years, vividly capturing portraits and landscapes in oils, charcoal, and pastels. He is 70 percent deaf. He is also legally blind.

If you're sitting for a portrait and Tim looks you in the eye, he cannot see your mouth. Instead of taking in the whole scene, he scans his subject bit by bit, memorizing as many details as he can, then he fills in from memory what his eyes leave out. "A good painting is a lot of good decisions," he explains.

The symptoms of Tim's genetic condition, Usher syndrome, appeared early. At five, Tim was wearing hearing aids full-time. By high school, when he was walking around at night, a friend would say "duck" so he didn't run into tree branches. Finally, when Tim turned thirty, an eye doctor referred him to a specialist, who diagnosed his condition. He also informed Tim there was no cure. The doctor's recommendation was blunt: "You'd better find another profession."

After this discouraging advice, Tim struggled with sometimes-paralyzing fear and frequent nightmares. Once, after he spent two hours finishing a charcoal portrait, his son walked in and asked, "What's with the purple?" Tim could no longer see the difference between purple and gray. Searching for other ways to use his knowledge, he began teaching art classes online. He received glowing reviews and students halfway around the world started waking up at two a.m. to learn from him. Tim and his wife Kim expanded these classes into an online school. One day Kim watched a talk Adam gave on resilience and felt like he was describing her husband. She emailed Adam to explain that Tim was "the most persevering person I have ever had the privilege to know."

Adam wondered where Tim got his resilience. Tim said it began with his parents. Tim's dad had a knack for reframing painful events. One day Tim came home from school upset that kids were staring and asking what was in his ear. His father gave him a tip: next time it happened, Tim could press his hearing aid, throw a punch in the air, and shout, "Yes! Cubs are up two to one in the ninth." Tim gave it a try, and the kids were jealous that he was listening to the game during a boring class. In high school, Tim leaned in for a kiss at the end of a date and his hearing aid started beeping loudly. His father told him not to worry about it: "She's probably saying to her mom right now, 'I kissed boys before tonight and I've seen fireworks—but I've never heard sirens.'"

Tim followed his dad's advice and learned to respond to embarrassment with humor. He discovered that his own reaction to his disability influenced how others reacted, which meant he could control how he was perceived. Reframing these moments became second nature. "It was a blessing to have a dad who turned times when you're feeling stupid into 'You become stronger as you seek solutions to seeming roadblocks or dead ends,'" he said.

When Dave died, my biggest concern was that my children's happiness would be destroyed. My childhood friend Mindy Levy lost her mother to suicide when we were thirteen. I slept in Mindy's room that night and held her as she cried. More than thirty years later, she was the first friend I called from the hospital in Mexico. I screamed into the phone hysterically, "Tell me my kids are going to be okay. Tell me they'll be okay!" At first, Mindy couldn't figure out what had happened. Once she did, she told me what she truly believed: my children would be okay. In that moment, nothing could have consoled me, but I knew Mindy grew up to be a loving and happy adult. Having seen her recover helped me believe that my daughter and son could too.

After the flight home—hours I can barely remember—my mom and sister met me at the airport, tears streaming down their faces, their bodies supporting me as I got into the car. My worst nightmare had never included the conversation I was about to have. How do you tell a seven- and ten-year-old that they will never see their father again?

On the way back from Mexico, Marne had reminded me that a close friend of ours, Carole Geithner, was a social worker who counseled grieving children. I called Carole on the agonizing car ride home. She suggested that I first let my kids know that I had very sad news and then tell them what had happened simply and directly. She said it was important to reassure them that many parts of their lives would be just like before: they still had the rest of their family, they would still go to school with their friends. She told me to follow their lead and answer their questions and that they might ask if I was going to die too. I was grateful she had prepared me for this since it was one of my daughter's first questions. Carole advised me not to make a false promise to them that I would live forever, but rather explain to them that it was very unusual for someone to die so young. Mostly, she told me to say over and over that I loved them and we would get through this together.

When I walked in the house, my daughter greeted me as if nothing was out of the ordinary. "Hi, Mom," she said and headed upstairs to her room. I was frozen to the floor. My son immediately realized something was wrong. "Why are you home?" he asked. "And where's Dad?" We all sat down on the couch with my parents and my sister. My heart was pounding so loudly that I could barely hear my own voice. With my father's strong arm around my shoulders, trying to protect me as he always has, I found the courage to speak: "I have terrible news. Terrible. Daddy died."

The screaming and crying that followed haunt me to this day—primal screams and cries that echoed the ones in my heart. Nothing has come close to the pain of this moment. Even now when my mind wanders back, I shake and my throat constricts. Still, as truly horrific as this was, we got through it. I would never wish for anyone to gain this perspective—but perspective it is.

While they suffered an irreparable loss, my children are still fortunate. Nothing will bring their father back, but our circumstances have softened the blow. This is not the case for many children facing heartbreaking difficulties. Poverty rates for children are one in six in Australia, one in five in the U.K. and the U.S., and three in five in South Africa. In the U.S., one-third of black and close to one-third of Latino children are poor, and forty-three percent of children of single mothers live in poverty. More than two and a half million American children have a parent in jail. Many children face serious illness, neglect, abuse, or homelessness. These extreme levels of harm and deprivation can impede children's intellectual, social, emotional, and academic development.

We owe all children safety, support, opportunity, and help finding a way forward, especially in the most tragic situations. Early and comprehensive intervention is critical. At "trauma-sensitive schools" like the Primary School in East Palo Alto, the staff is trained to recognize the effects of toxic stress on children. When kids misbehave, instead of being blamed, shamed, or severely punished, they are made to feel safe so that they can learn. These schools also offer mental health and crisis support services for children and coaching for their parents.

High-quality preschool education is known to improve children's cognitive development, and providing support even earlier makes a difference. All around the United States, the Nurse-Family Partnership has proven through rigorous experiments how valuable investing in children can be. When disadvantaged families are provided with home visits and counseling from the start of pregnancy until the kids turn two, over the next decade and a half there are 79 percent fewer cases of child abuse and neglect. By the time these children turn fifteen, on average they are arrested half as often as their peers, and their mothers receive cash assistance benefits for thirty fewer months. Programs like this help build resilience within families. Along with being the correct moral choice, these investments make economic sense too: every dollar put into these visits yields about $5.70 in benefits.

We all want to raise resilient kids so they can overcome obstacles big and small. Resilience leads to greater happiness, more success, and better health. As I learned from Adam—and as Tim's dad knew instinctively—resilience is not a fixed personality trait. It's a lifelong project.

Building resilience depends on the opportunities children have and the relationships they form with parents, caregivers, teachers, and friends. We can start by helping children develop four core beliefs: (1) they have some control over their lives; (2) they can learn from failure; (3) they matter as human beings; and (4) they have real strengths to rely on and share.

These four beliefs have a real impact on kids. One study tracked hundreds of at-risk children for three decades. They grew up in environments with severe poverty, alcohol abuse, or mental illness, and two out of three developed serious problems by adolescence and adulthood. Yet despite these extreme hardships, a third of the kids matured into "competent, confident, and caring young adults" with no record of delinquency or mental health problems. These resilient children shared something: they felt a strong sense of control over their lives. They saw themselves as the masters of their own fate and viewed negative events not as threats but as challenges and even opportunities. The same holds true for children who aren't at risk: the most resilient ones realize they have the power to shape their own lives. Their caregivers communicate clear and consistent expectations, giving them structure and predictability, which increases their sense of control.

Kathy Andersen showed me how powerful control can be. I first met Kathy through her heroic efforts to rescue teenage victims of sex trafficking and exploitation in Miami. Kathy created a program called Change Your Shoes that helps young women see that the trauma in their past does not determine their future. "They feel they have limited choices," Kathy says. "Like me, most of them have been abused, and that abuse makes you feel like you have no control over your own life. My goal is to show them that they have the power to step out of their shoes—step out of everything that holds them back. They can take little steps every day to make their lives better. I try to inspire them to put on the shoes they want to walk in and know that they still have choices to make."

I joined Kathy at a group meeting in the living room of a drop-in center, where I met Johanacheka "Jay" Francois, a fifteen-year-old mother who was holding her new baby on her lap. Jay described the horrors of being abused at home, running away, and becoming a victim of sex trafficking. I saw how Kathy responded, sharing her own story—how she had been abused by her adoptive father, run away from home, and survived a suicide attempt. Kathy told the girls that her life turned around once she realized that her only way out was to get an education.

Kathy asked the girls to share their dreams. One said she wanted to be an artist. Another said she wanted to be a lawyer to help girls like her. A third wanted to run a nonprofit to provide shelter to girls in need. Jay said that her dream was to be a great mother. Kathy then asked the girls to write down the goals that would allow them to achieve those dreams. All of them wrote down the same thing: they would need to finish school. Next, Kathy asked them to share what they would have to do today—and the next day and the next day— to reach that goal. "Get better grades," one said. "Find a high school to go to and register," said another. "Commit to study," said Jay. Since then, Jay has defied the odds by finishing high school and starting college. "I feel like now my future is in my hands," she says. "It's all about being a great mother for my daughter and giving her a good future."

The second belief that shapes children's resilience is that they can learn from failure. Psychologist Carol Dweck has shown that children respond better to adversity when they have a growth mindset instead of a fixed one. A fixed mindset means viewing abilities as something we're either born with or not: "I'm a whiz at math but don't have the drama gene." When kids have a growth mindset, they see abilities as skills that can be learned and developed. They can work to improve. "I may not be a natural actor, but if I rehearse enough I can shine on the stage."

Whether children develop a fixed or growth mindset depends in part on the type of praise they receive from parents and teachers. Dweck's team randomly assigned students to receive different kinds of positive feedback after they took a test. The kids who were praised for being smart did worse on later tests because they viewed their intelligence as a fixed attribute. When the "smart" ones struggled, they decided that they just didn't have the ability. Instead of attempting to complete a more difficult test, they gave up. But when kids were praised for trying, they worked harder on the challenging test and made more of an effort to finish it.

Dweck and her collaborators have shown that growth mindsets can be taught relatively quickly and with remarkable effects. After students at risk of dropping out of high school completed an online exercise emphasizing that skills can be developed, their academic performance improved. When college freshmen completed this same exercise during orientation, the dropout risk among black, Latino, and first-generation students decreased by 46 percent. Their academic struggles seemed less personal and permanent, and the students became as likely to stay in school as those from other backgrounds. When coupled with high-quality education and long-term support, programs like this can have a lasting impact.

Today the importance of helping kids develop a growth mindset is widely recognized but poorly practiced. There's a knowing-doing gap: many parents and teachers understand the idea but do not always succeed in applying it. Despite my best efforts, I am sometimes one of those parents. When my daughter does well on a test, I still find myself blurting out, "Great job!" rather than, "I'm glad you tried your hardest." In *How to Raise an Adult,* former Stanford dean Julie Lythcott-Haims advises parents to teach children that difficulties are how we grow. She calls this "normalizing struggle." When parents treat failure as an opportunity to learn rather than an embarrassment to be avoided, kids are more likely to take on challenges. When a kid struggles at math, instead of saying, "Maybe math isn't one of your strengths," Dweck recommends, "The feeling of math being hard is the feeling of your brain growing."

The third belief that affects children's resilience is mattering: knowing that other people notice you, care about you, and rely on you. Many parents communicate this naturally. They listen closely to their children, show that they value their ideas, and help them create strong, secure attachments with others. In a study of more than two thousand adolescents between the ages of eleven and eighteen, many of whom faced severe adversity, those who felt they mattered were less likely to have low self-esteem, depression, and suicidal thoughts.

Mattering is often a challenge for children in stigmatized groups. LGBTQ youths face high rates of bullying and harassment and many lack support from adults at home or at school. Lesbian, gay, and bisexual youths are four times more likely than their peers to attempt suicide, and a quarter of transgender youths report having tried to kill themselves. Thanks to the Trevor Project, LGBTQ youths have 24/7 access to free counseling by text and phone. Mat Herman, who was a trained volunteer on the Trevor hotline, emphasized that knowing someone cares—even if it's a stranger—can offer a lifeline. "We'd get callers who were fourteen and scared and they just needed to know someone was out there and they weren't alone," he explained. "It's clichéd but that's what it was." During the four years that Mat answered calls with a warm hello, he often heard the click of a hang-up before callers said a word. Like in the experiment where people knew they could stop blasts of noise by pressing a button, when youths called and hung up, it was as if they were checking to see if the button was working. Over time, many would respond to the comforting voice by finding the courage to start a conversation. "There were so many repeat callers—you become like a friend to them," Mat said.

For children, it often takes adults to show them that they matter. A friend of mine's son has struggled with anxiety and depression from an early age. One day at camp he made a robot. The next morning he found that bullies had trashed it. A kid said to him, "You're worthless." The message was clear: his work didn't matter and neither did he. He didn't want to play baseball or interact with other kids at school because he felt like they were making fun of him. "He'd put his hoodie on and sit in the back in his own world," his mother told me.

A turning point came when one of his former teachers started spending time with him every week. Progress happened little by little as she helped him reach out to other kids and make friends. She offered tips: join a group that's playing games during lunch, email classmates and invite them to come over or go to a movie. The teacher then followed up, reinforcing each step he took; she gave him control but also made it clear that she was looking out for him. She cared. He mattered. When a new kid started at the school, the teacher encouraged them to get together. The two boys connected over a card game and the friendship took.

"It was like the sun came out in our house," his mom told me, adding, "There's no easy answer. I'm glad we found the combination of things that helped, including medication. But it made such a difference for a teacher to take an interest in him and a friend to bond with him." Mattering was a counterweight to the external bullying and internal anxiety.

In Denmark, mattering is part of the school curriculum. During a weekly hour called Klassen Time, students come together to discuss problems and help one another. Danish children do this every week from age six until they graduate from high school. To sweeten the deal, each week a different student brings cake. When children present their own problems, they feel listened to, and when their classmates seek guidance, they feel they can make a difference. The children learn empathy by hearing others' perspectives and reflecting on how their behavior affects those around them. They are taught to think, "How do others feel? And how do my actions make them feel?"

The fourth belief held by resilient kids is that they have strengths they can rely on and share with others. In some of the poorest areas of India, a resilience program called Girls First has improved the mental and physical health of adolescent girls. In 2009, Girls First started with a pilot project in the state of Bihar, where 95 percent of women have less than twelve years of education and almost 70 percent are pregnant by age eighteen. The program teaches girls to identify and practice different strengths of character—from courage to creativity, justice to kindness, humility to gratitude. Girls who attended just one hour a week over six months saw their emotional resilience climb. During one session, an eighth grader named Ritu learned that bravery was one of her strengths. Soon afterward, she intervened to stop a boy from harassing her friends, and when her father tried to make her ninth-grade sister get married, Ritu spoke up and convinced him to wait.

Girls First is run by Steve Leventhal, who emerged unscathed from a serious car accident at the time his wife was expecting their first child. "I had one of those near-death experiences you read about," Steve told us. "I realized I could die even before my daughter was born and it changed me." After his daughter's birth, Steve felt so grateful that he wanted to help other children, so he took the reins of CorStone, a struggling nonprofit, and focused on building programs like Girls First. His goal that first year was to help one hundred girls in India. Six years later, the program has helped fifty thousand. "Our work is to turn on a light," Steve reflects. "The girls often say that no one had ever told them they had strengths."

Helping children identify strengths can be critical after traumatic events. One of Adam's undergraduate students at Wharton, Kayvon Asemani, was nine years old when his father violently assaulted his mother, leaving her brain-dead. Remarkably, Kayvon was able to persevere. "Although I lost my mother," Kayvon says, "I never lost her faith in me." She had taught her son that he mattered. A friend's father reinforced that belief and helped Kayvon apply to the school that had changed his own life. The Milton Hershey School's mission is to give children the very best education regardless of their financial circumstances. At Hershey, Kayvon had access to great teachers and the opportunity to pursue higher education: the school would pay for any college tuition that financial aid did not cover.

Teachers helped Kayvon discover and develop his strengths. One encouraged him to start playing the trombone. Music became his salvation, giving him hope that he could live a life that would have made his mother proud. By middle school, Kayvon was ranked as one of the best trombone players in his district. But when he started high school, he was bullied. As one of the shortest boys in his grade, he was an easy target. Upperclassmen beat him up, made fun of him in the hallways, and spread rumors about him. When he rapped at a pep rally, they booed him off the stage.

When the next freshman class entered, Kayvon found the strength to stand up for himself and others. He welcomed the new students and offered support to those who were being bullied. He shared his rap music with them. By his senior year, many students knew his songs by heart. He was elected student body president and graduated as valedictorian. "Music taught me how to bounce back from challenges more than anything else in this world," Kayvon told us. "Whether it's the tragedy that tore my family apart or being bullied or something as silly as a high school breakup, it channeled my energy into something positive. Music transforms the darkness."

Like their students, teachers benefit from a growth mindset. Since the 1960s, researchers have demonstrated that when teachers are told students from stigmatized groups have potential to bloom, the teachers begin to treat them differently. They help students learn from failure. They set high expectations, give students extra attention, and actively encourage them to develop their strengths. This can help students believe in themselves and work harder, earning higher grades.

With the right support, beliefs can fuel action and become self-fulfilling. Believe you can learn from failure and you become less defensive and more open. Believe you matter and you spend more time helping others, which helps you matter even more. Believe you have strengths and you start seeing opportunities to use them. Believe you are a wizard who can cross the space-time continuum and you may have gone too far.

When kids face trauma, the beliefs that help build resilience become even more critical. More than 1.8 million children in America have lost a parent, and in a national poll nearly three-quarters said their lives would have been "much better" if their parent had survived. When asked whether they would trade a year of their lives for just one more day with their late mother or father, more than half said yes.

In our house, we know that feeling well. My kids were heart-broken. I was heartbroken—and I was heartbroken that they were heartbroken. But even in those dark hours when my children first learned that their lives had changed forever, there were glimpses of light. My son stopped crying for a moment to thank me for coming home to be with him when he found out, and to thank my sister and parents for being there too. *Amazing.* Later that night when I was putting my daughter to bed, she said, "I am not only sad for us, Mommy. I am sad for Grandma Paula and Uncle Rob because they lost him too." *Amazing.* I remembered how the night Mindy's mom died, she asked me to sleep over but then worried that our other friends would feel left out. Even in the worst moments of their lives, my kids—like Mindy—had the capacity to think of others. And that gave me hope.

A few days later, my kids and I sat down with a big piece of paper and colored markers. Over the years, we had hung signs and schedules over their backpack cubbies. Carole had explained that giving kids a sense of stability was essential at a time when their world is turned upside down. I thought it might help to create "family rules," which we could put on the wall to remind us of the coping mechanisms we would need. We sat down to write them out together.

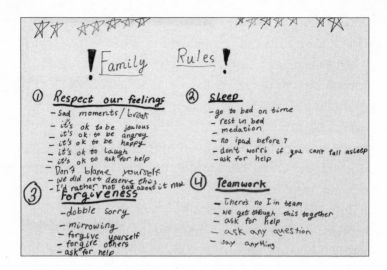

I wanted them to know that they should respect their feelings and not try to suppress them. We wrote together that it's okay to be sad and they could take breaks from any activity to cry. That it's okay to be angry and jealous of their friends and cousins who still had fathers. That it's okay to say to anyone that they did not want to talk about it now. That they should know we did not deserve this. I wanted to make sure guilt did not cloud any moment when my kids could have a break from grief, so we agreed that it was okay to be happy and to laugh.

People often marvel at how resilient kids can be. There are neurological reasons for this: kids have more neural plasticity than adults, allowing their brains to adapt more easily in the face of stress. I learned from Carole that children have limits to how much intense emotion they can process at once. They have shorter "feeling spans"; their grief comes more in bursts than in sustained periods. Kids also sometimes express their grief through behavior changes and play rather than in words. As Carole told me to expect, my children cycled in and out of grief very quickly, sobbing one moment and then running off to play the next.

I realized sleep would be important to help us get through this. When I was a child, my parents always emphasized sleep, which I thought was *no fun at all*. Once I had my own children, I understood how right they were. When we're tired, we're physically and mentally weaker, more likely to be irritable, and we literally lack the energy to feel joy. Sleep matters even more in adversity because we need to marshal all our strength, so I stuck as close as I could to their regular bedtimes. When my kids had trouble falling asleep, I tried to teach them to count six breaths in and out, just as my mom had taught me.

Since our feelings were extremely raw, I knew we would make many mistakes, so forgiveness became a huge theme. The year before, my daughter and I had attended a Girls Leadership workshop and learned about "fast double-sorries"— when two people hurt each other's feelings, you both apologize quickly so that you forgive each other and yourselves. Feeling deep grief and anger meant we all got upset much more easily, so we relied on this strategy a lot. When we lost control of our emotions, we would say we were sorry right away. Then we would "mirror" each other: the first person would explain what was upsetting, and the second person would repeat it back and apologize. We were trying to show that the other person's feelings mattered to us. At one point, my daughter cried out, "I'm upset because both of you got more years with Daddy than I did." My son and I acknowledged that it was unfair that she'd had the least time.

I tried to help my children be kind to themselves. To not beat themselves up for being angry at each other, for being jealous of other kids and even me because I still had a father. I came to see teaching them self-compassion as part of nurturing a growth mindset. When they didn't dwell on yesterday's grief, they could approach today as a new day. We vowed to do this, like everything else, as a team.

It didn't always work as planned. Long before Dave died I had learned that parenting was the most humbling job in the world—and now I had to relearn how to do it alone. My kids were struggling with their emotions and so was I, which made even the most basic decisions hard. Dave and I were always strict about bedtimes—but do you put an exhausted child to bed on time when he is crying for his lost father? When small issues become big fights, do you hold children to the same behavioral standards as before, or do you overlook these outbursts because you feel that same anger? And if you let things slide too much, will the kids act out with their friends, who are not old enough to understand and forgive? I wavered back and forth and made a lot of mistakes. A lot.

Once again, I was so grateful for my friends and family. I relied on my mom and her friend Merle for parenting advice and tried to follow their suggestions. Say things once. Stay calm. Sometimes, no matter how carefully I planned how to handle a situation, I failed. One day my daughter refused to leave the house for a group hike with Marne, Phil, Mark, and Priscilla. While the others waited outside, I tried to convince her that she'd have fun, but she wouldn't budge. Literally. She sat down on the floor, and I couldn't get her to move. I became, I believe the clinical term is, "super frustrated." Phil came in to check on our progress and found the two of us sitting on the floor sobbing. With humor, he cajoled my daughter into getting back on her feet and joining the group. Priscilla cajoled me into doing the same. A short time later, after double-sorries, my daughter was running up a hiking path, smiling.

The family rules still hang above the kids' cubbies, but only recently did I notice that asking for help is in all four categories. Now I see that this is at the heart of building resilience. When children feel comfortable asking for help, they know they matter. They see that others care and want to be there for them.

They understand that they are not alone and can gain some control by reaching out for support. They realize that pain is not permanent; things can get better. Carole helped me understand that even when I felt helpless because I could not fix or cure my children's grief, if I could walk alongside them and listen—what she called "companioning"—I would be helping them.

As I wrestled with my own emotions, I worried about how much of my grief to show my children. For the first few months, we were all crying constantly. One day my son told me it made him sad when I cried, so I began holding back my tears, running up to my bedroom and closing the door when I felt them well up. Initially it seemed to help. But a few days later my son asked me in anger, "Why don't you miss Daddy anymore?" By protecting him from my tears, I had stopped modeling the behavior I wanted from him. I apologized for hiding my emotions and started letting him see them again.

Since the day Dave died, I have continued to talk about him. It's not always easy to do and I've watched adults flinch, as if it's too painful for *them* to be reminded. But I have a deep desire to keep Dave's memory alive, and when I mention him he remains present. Because our children were so young, I realize—and this completely breaks my heart—that their memories of their father will fade, so it's up to me to make sure they know him.

A friend of mine who lost her father when she was six years old told me that she has spent her adult life trying to piece together who he really was, so I asked dozens of Dave's closest family members, friends, and colleagues to capture their memories of him on video. My daughter and son will never have another conversation with their father, but one day when they are ready they will learn about him from those who loved him. I also taped my children sharing their own memories, so that as they grow up they will know which memories of him are truly theirs. This past Thanksgiving my daughter was distraught, and when I got her to open up she told me, "I'm forgetting Daddy because I haven't seen him for so long." I showed her a video of her talking about him and it helped.

When children grow up with a strong understanding of their family's history—where their grandparents grew up, what their parents' childhoods were like—they have better coping skills and a stronger sense of belonging. Talking openly about positive and even difficult memories can help develop resilience. It's especially powerful to share stories about how the family sticks together through good times and bad, which allows kids to feel that they are connected to something larger than themselves. Just as journaling can help adults process adversity, these discussions help children make sense of their past and embrace challenges. Giving all members of the family a chance to tell their stories builds self-esteem, particularly for girls. And making sure to integrate different perspectives into a coherent story builds a sense of control, particularly for boys.

A friend who lost his mother when he was young told me that over time she no longer seemed real. People either were afraid to mention his mom or spoke of her in idealized terms. I try to hold on to Dave as he really was: loving, generous, brilliant, funny, and also pretty clumsy. He would spill things constantly and was always shocked when he did. Now when emotions are swirling yet my son stays calm, I tell him, "You are just like your daddy." When my daughter stands up for a classmate who is getting picked on, I say, "Just like your daddy." And when either of them knocks a glass over, I say it too.

Parents often worry that these conversations will make their children sad, but research on nostalgia suggests the opposite. "Nostalgia" comes from the Greek words *nostos* and *algos,* which mean "return" and "pain." Nostalgia is literally the suffering that we feel when we yearn for the past to come back to us, yet psychologists find that it is mostly a pleasant state. After people reflect on an event, they tend to feel happier and more connected to others. They often find life more meaningful and become inspired to create a better future. Rather than ignoring painful milestones from the past, we try to mark them in the present. My friend Devon Spurgeon lost her father young and gave me a wonderful idea for what would have been Dave's forty-eighth birthday—my kids and I wrote letters to Dave and sent them up in balloons.

I've noticed that when people tell stories about Dave, my son and daughter are usually comforted. My brother-in-law Marc has told them Dave had a "happy energy" and shared it generously: "It's hard to imagine your dad having a good time without lots of other people joining in." Phil often comments to our kids that Dave didn't brag or exaggerate but spoke to others thoughtfully and with care. We all wish that they had Dave to show them how to be happy and humble by his example. Instead, we are trying to make the most of Option B.

Adam told me about a program at Arizona State University that helps children recover after losing parents. One of its key steps is to create a new family identity so kids feel that the people left make a complete unit. Looking back at the photos of the three of us taken even in those first weeks and months, I was surprised to see that we did have some moments of happiness— like when my son and daughter played tag with friends. Photos are important because happiness is remembered, not just experienced. And losing Dave taught me how precious video is: when I see photos of him, I long to see him move and hear him speak. Now I take videos as much as possible. My kids used to duck whenever I began recording them, but since they started watching these clips to remember their father, they smile and talk to the camera.

The Arizona State program also recommends setting aside time for the new family unit to have fun together. It gives kids a break from grief and helps them feel like they're part of a whole family again. The activity can't be passive like watching TV; it has to be something active like playing board games or cooking together. We called it FAF, which is short for "Family Awesome Fun." My son offered to let my daughter choose the first activity, and FAF became a weekly tradition we stuck to for more than a year. We also created a family cheer where we link arms and shout, "We are strong!"

The three of us are still adjusting to being just the three of us. There are still plenty of fast double-sorries as we continue to cope and learn and make mistakes and grow. As individuals, we feel weaker on some days than on others. But as a family we are stronger together.

Nearly a year after Dave died, I attended my son's music concert at school one afternoon. As hard as I try not to be jealous of others, seeing all the fathers watching their children was a stark reminder of what my children and I lost—and what Dave lost. As soon as I got home, I ran upstairs in tears. Unfortunately, my workday wasn't over; I had to host the annual dinner for Facebook's largest clients from around the world. As people started arriving, I still couldn't pull myself together. My son was with me, and I told him that I needed to stop crying and go downstairs. He held my hand and said, "You should just go. And it's okay if you're crying. Everyone knows what happened to us." Then he added, "Mom, they probably have things they cry about too, so you should just be yourself."

He was teaching me what I had tried to teach him.

8

Finding Strength Together

We are caught in an inescapable network of mutuality,
tied in a single garment of destiny. Whatever affects
one directly affects all indirectly.

—MARTIN LUTHER KING JR.

IN 1972, a plane flying from Uruguay to Chile crashed into a mountain in the Andes, split in half, and barreled down a snowy slope. For the thirty-three survivors, this was just the beginning of an extraordinary ordeal. Over the next seventy-two days, the group battled shock, frostbite, avalanches, and starvation. Only sixteen of them made it out. *Alive.*

Thanks to the popular book and movie, many of us know the extreme measures taken by the group in order to survive. New analysis by Spencer Harrison—a researcher, mountain climber, and colleague of Adam's—explains not just *how* these men survived, but *why*. Spencer tracked down four of the survivors, combed through their journals, and even visited the crash site with one of them. Every survivor's story shared a common theme: a key to their resilience was hope.

Most of the forty-five people on board were rugby players

in their late teens and early twenties traveling to an exhibition match. Damage to the plane's radio meant they could not send communications, but they could still receive them. Their first plan was to wait for rescue in the shelter of the plane. "We all believed that rescue was our only chance of survival," Nando Parrado wrote, "and we clung to that hope with an almost religious zeal." Nine days later, their supplies were depleted. The group was forced to turn to their only remaining source of food: the flesh from the frozen bodies of their teammates who had died. The next morning, a few of the passengers heard over the radio that the search had been called off. "We mustn't tell them," said the team captain. "At least let them go on hoping." Another passenger, Gustavo Nicolich, disagreed. "Good news!" he shouted. "We're going to get out of here on our own."

We normally think of hope as something individuals hold in their heads and in their hearts. But people can build hope together. By creating a shared identity, individuals can form a group that has a past and a brighter future.

"Some people say, 'If there's life, there's hope,'" survivor Roberto Canessa explained. "But for us, it was the opposite: 'If there's hope, there's life.'" During long, cold, and hungry days, the crash survivors prayed together. They planned projects to launch after returning to civilization: one passenger spoke of opening a restaurant, another dreamed of having a farm. Each night, two of the survivors looked at the moon and imagined that right then their parents were looking at the same moon. Another took pictures to record their plight. Many wrote letters to their families declaring their will to live. "To maintain faith at all times, despite our setbacks, we had to become alchemists," survivor Javier Methol said. "Changing tragedy into a miracle, depression into hope."

Of course hope by itself isn't enough. Many of the passengers had hope yet still lost their lives. But hope keeps people from giving in to despair. Researchers find that hope springs up and persists when "communities of people generate new images of possibility." Believing in new possibilities helps people fight back against the idea of permanence and propels them to seek out new options; they find the will and the way to move forward. Psychologists call this "grounded hope"—the understanding that if you take action you can make things better. "I never stopped praying for the arrival of our rescuers, or for the intercession of God," Parrado recalled. "But at the same time the cold-blooded voice that had urged me to save my tears was always whispering in the back of my mind: 'No one will find us. We will die here. We must make a plan. We must save ourselves.'"

Parrado and Canessa set out on a trek with a third survivor and nearly froze to death before locating the tail of the plane, which contained insulation that they turned into a sleeping bag. Nearly two months after the crash, this makeshift sleeping bag allowed Parrado and Canessa to launch another expedition. They hiked thirty-three miles across treacherous terrain, scaling a 14,000-foot peak. After ten days, they spotted a man on horseback. The fourteen other survivors were rescued by helicopter.

The community formed by the *Alive* survivors has stayed close for decades. Each year they gather on the anniversary of their rescue to play rugby. Together they contributed to a book about their experience, *La Sociedad de la Nieve—The Snow Society*. And in 2010, when thirty-three miners were trapped underground in Chile, four of the Andes survivors flew in from Uruguay to address the miners by video. "We've come to give them a little faith and hope," Gustavo Servino said at the time. "To say we're at their service if they need us for anything. And above all, to give support to the families outside." After sixty-nine days, the first miner was lifted to the surface in a capsule while hundreds cheered. It took a full day, but all thirty-three miners were rescued and reunited with their loved ones. The tent city where everyone gathered above the mine was called Campamento Esperanza (Camp Hope).

Resilience is not just built in individuals. It is built *among* individuals—in our neighborhoods, schools, towns, and governments. When we build resilience together, we become stronger ourselves and form communities that can overcome obstacles and prevent adversity. Collective resilience requires more than just shared hope—it is also fueled by shared experiences, shared narratives, and shared power.

For my children and me, getting to know people who also lost a parent or a spouse has provided much-needed comfort. In most religions and cultures, traditions around mourning are communal; we come together to bury and remember those we have lost. At first, our house was filled with friends and family who made sure we had support around the clock. But eventually our loved ones needed to get back to their normal routines and we needed to find a new normal routine—and the loneliness hit hard.

In my second week of widowhood, I had put my kids to bed and was sitting alone in my kitchen when I flashed forward to an image I'd never thought of before: a much older version of myself sitting at that same table in front of a Scrabble board. But instead of Dave sitting across from me, I was staring at an empty chair. That week, my kids and I went to Kara, a local grief support center. Meeting other people who were farther along in the same journey helped us overcome permanence by showing us that we wouldn't be stuck in the void of acute grief forever. "When we suffer loss or face difficulties of any kind, there is a real desire deep in most people for human connection," explained Kara's executive director Jim Santucci, who himself lost a child. "Support groups connect you with others who really get what you are going through. Deep human connection. It is not just 'Oh, I feel bad for you' but 'I actually understand.'"

My kids also attended Experience Camps, a free weeklong program for children who have lost a parent, sibling, or primary caregiver. Two of the core values at the camp are building community and inspiring hope. In one exercise, kids went to stations to confront an emotion associated with grieving. For anger, kids used chalk to scrawl words that made them angry on the pavement. Some wrote "bullying"; others wrote "cancer" or "drugs." Then on the count of three they threw water balloons on the ground to smear the words away and release their anger. At a second station, a camper held a brick representing guilt. As the brick became too heavy, another camper shared the burden of its weight. These exercises helped show my children that their emotions were normal and other kids felt them too.

To join a community after tragedy, we often have to accept our new—and often unwelcome—identity. Writer Allen Rucker told us that after he became paralyzed, "I initially didn't want to hang around people who were in wheelchairs. I didn't want to belong to that club. I saw myself as a freak; I didn't want to join the freak fraternity." His mind didn't change overnight. "It took four or five years. It almost felt like every cell in my brain had to transfer, one at a time, very slowly learning to accept this thing." As he made this personal adjustment, he grew closer to those who understood his situation. The bonus, he told us, was "these are some of the funniest people I have ever met because their humor is just as dark as possible."

Allen's point struck a deep chord within me. It took me a long time to say the word "widow," and to this day it makes me wince. Still, I am a widow and accepting this identity allowed me to form new friendships. In the past two years, all of the new friends I've made have lived through tragedy. (The first time I wrote that sentence it said, "most have lived through tragedy," but then I realized it was literally all of them.) The club that no one wants to belong to is incredibly bonding. Perhaps because none of us wanted to join, we cling to one another.

When Steven Czifra arrived at the University of California, Berkeley, he felt like an outsider—and not just because at thirty-eight he was twice as old as a typical freshman. Growing up, Steven suffered physical abuse and started smoking crack at age ten. Burglaries and carjacking led to stints in juvenile hall and then state prison. After fighting with another inmate and spitting on a guard, Steven was sent to solitary confinement *for four years*. He has since testified to the California State Legislature that isolation is a "torture chamber."

After his release from prison, Steven entered a twelve-step program, completed his GED, and met his partner Sylvia. He discovered a love of English literature, and after several years at community college he was accepted to Berkeley. He'd earned his spot, but once he got to campus he felt different and disconnected. "I went to the English classes, but I didn't really see myself in the faces of the people there," he said. Then one day Steven was walking through the center for transfer students and was stopped by Danny Murillo, another student in his thirties, who said he instantly recognized Steven's "demeanor." Within a minute, they realized that they'd both spent time in solitary at Pelican Bay State Prison. "What happened in that moment," Steven said, "is I saw myself as a student at Cal with every privilege and every right to be there."

Steven and Danny became close friends and united to speak out against the cruelty of solitary confinement. They also helped start the Underground Scholars Initiative, a group that supports Berkeley students affected by incarceration. Having experienced the deepest desolation, they wanted to come together as a community. "As a collective of students, we wanted to put each other in the best possible position to succeed," Danny told us. "A lot of times formerly incarcerated people don't want to ask for help. We're trying to get them to understand that it's actually a sign of strength to recognize when you don't have the skills to do something—and reach out for help. Wanting to improve is not a sign of weakness."

The Posse Foundation is another organization founded on the importance of grouping students with similar backgrounds to combat feelings of isolation. Posse took its name from a remark made by a talented but lonely former student who observed, "If I only had my posse with me, I never would've dropped out." Posse recruits underprivileged high schoolers who have demonstrated extraordinary academic and leadership potential and sends them in teams of ten to attend the same college on scholarship. Since 1989, Posse has helped nearly seven thousand students attend college with a 90 percent graduation rate. If we are serious about creating ladders of opportunity for everyone, we need to provide greater public and private support for long-term, intensive efforts like Posse.

Along with shared hope and experiences, shared narratives can build collective resilience. Narratives might sound "light"—how important can a story be?—but they are how we explain our past and set expectations for our future. Just as family stories help children feel a sense of belonging, collective stories create identity for communities. And stories that emphasize values like equality are critical for pursuing justice.

Shared stories are often created by rewriting old narratives and countering unfair stereotypes. In the United States and around the world, girls are often expected to be worse at math than boys. When college students were reminded of their gender before taking a math test, women performed 43 percent worse than men. When the exact same test was called a "problem-solving test" instead of a "math test," the gender gap in performance vanished. In another experiment, black students scored lower than white students after being told that a test would assess their verbal ability, but when ability wasn't mentioned, the race gap in performance disappeared.

Psychologists call this "stereotype threat": the fear of being reduced to a negative stereotype. That fear becomes a self-fulfilling prophecy when anxiety disrupts our thinking and causes us to conform to the stereotype. This effect undermines people of many races, religions, genders, sexual orientations, and backgrounds, and this is where the Posse Foundation rewrites the narrative. When Posse students arrive at college together, they create a different image on campus. In the words of one Posse alum, "The buzz around the school is that these Posse kids are cool and smart." Instead of being threatened by negative stereotypes, they are lifted by positive ones.

I gained a new appreciation for communities forming to change narratives years before when I was writing *Lean In*. As I began talking to women about reaching for their ambitions, one common reaction was, "I want to lean in . . . but *how?*" Women have less access to the mentorship and sponsorship that are key to success in the workplace, but peer support can have a big impact. I teamed up with three women who were passionate about peer mentorship—Rachel Thomas, Gina Bianchini, and Debi Hemmeter—to launch Lean In Circles, small groups of peers who meet regularly to support and encourage one another. Today there are 32,000 Circles in 150 countries. More than half of all members report that their Circle helped them through a difficult time, and two-thirds say they are more likely to take on a new challenge after joining. I realize now that part of why Circles help women reach for their individual goals is because they build collective resilience.

The Millennial Latinas Circle in East Palo Alto connects older women and teenagers with a group goal of helping the young women—many of whom are teen mothers—get into and graduate from college. The Circle was founded by Guadalupe Valencia, who was forced to transfer to a different school after she became pregnant at sixteen. Many of the other adults in the group have personal and family histories of teen pregnancy too, and having seen its effects they are determined to write a new story for the next generation. "We all know what it is to live in a household where 'college' is a word that is not even said," Guadalupe told me. "But for the Millennial Latinas, we are clear: College is not an option. College is a must." Guadalupe has become a role model for the members: along with working full-time, she has followed her own mantra and gone back to school to finish her degree.

Often the people fighting injustice are themselves the victims of injustice. They have to find the hope and strength to overcome the adversity they face today in order to work for improvements tomorrow. From the end of apartheid to the development of vaccines, some of the world's greatest achievements have been rooted in personal tragedies. By helping people cope with difficult circumstances and then take action to alter those circumstances, collective resilience can foster real social change.

Some hardships result from centuries-old discrimination—the steady accumulation of injustice that threatens to crush even the most resilient among us. Others hit unexpectedly. When sudden violence strikes, it can shake our faith in humanity to its core. In these moments, it's hard to hold on to hope. Instead, we are justifiably filled with anger, frustration, and fear. That's why I was riveted when I read a Facebook post by journalist Antoine Leiris, whose wife Hélène was killed in a

2015 Paris terrorist attack. Just two days later he wrote, "On Friday night, you stole the life of an exceptional being, the love of my life, the mother of my son, but you will not have my hate. . . . I will not give you the satisfaction of hating you." He made a promise to defeat hate by not allowing it to affect his seventeen-month-old son: "We will play as we do every day, and all his life this little boy will defy you by being happy and free. Because you will not have his hate either."

When I started reading Antoine's post, I felt tremendous sorrow. But when I finished it, I was overcome by a tingling sensation in my chest and a lump in my throat. Adam told me there was a term for this (psychologists have a term for everything). "Moral elevation" describes the feeling of being uplifted by an act of uncommon goodness. Elevation brings out what Abraham Lincoln called "the better angels of our nature." Even in the face of atrocity, elevation leads us to look at our similarities instead of our differences. We see the potential for good in others and gain hope that we can survive and rebuild. We become inspired to express compassion and battle injustice. As Martin Luther King Jr. said, "Let no man pull you so low as to hate him."

The month after Dave died, a white supremacist gunned down a senior pastor and eight parishioners during their Wednesday Bible study at Emanuel African Methodist Episcopal Church in Charleston, South Carolina. I was reeling from my own loss, and seeing such senseless violence sank me deeper into despair.

Then I heard about the congregation's response. That week, relatives of the victims went to court to address the gunman who had murdered their loved ones. One by one they rejected his hatred. "You took something very precious away from me," said Nadine Collier, whose mother was killed. "I will never get to talk to her ever again. I will never be able to hold her again, but I forgive you, and have mercy on your soul. . . . You hurt me. You hurt a lot of people. If God forgives you, I forgive you." Instead of being consumed by hatred, the church members chose forgiveness, which allowed them to come together and stand against racism and violence. Four days after the shooting, the church doors opened for regular Sunday service. Five days later, President Barack Obama spoke at the funeral of Reverend Clementa C. Pinckney and led the congregation in singing "Amazing Grace."

"Mother Emanuel," as the church is known, is the oldest African Methodist Episcopal church in the South. Its congregations have endured laws forbidding black worship, a white mob burning down their building, and an earthquake. After every tragedy, they came together to rebuild, sometimes literally and always emotionally. As Reverend Joseph Darby, the presiding elder for a neighboring district, told us, "Their extension of grace is rooted in a long-standing coping mechanism passed down from people who had no option in many cases but to forgive and move on while still leaving the door open for justice to be done. It takes you past raw vengeance. Forgiveness clears your head to pursue justice."

On the Sunday after the 2015 shooting, church bells around the city tolled at ten a.m. for nine minutes—one minute for each victim. "What unites us is stronger than what divides us," pronounced Jermaine Watkins, a pastor from a local church. "To hatred, we say no way, not today. To racism, we say no way, not today. To division, we say no way, not today. To reconciliation, we say yes. To loss of hope, we say no way, not today. To a racial war, we say no way, not today. . . . Charleston, together, we say no way, not today." As the community began picking up the pieces, area churches started hosting conferences on preventing violence. After the FBI determined that a system breakdown had allowed the shooter to purchase a gun, families who had been affected by gun violence joined forces with church and political leaders to advocate for more rigorous background checks.

Social activism was not new to Charleston. Years before the shooting, religious leaders created the Charleston Area Justice Ministry—a network of twenty-seven faith-based congregations, including churches, synagogues, and a mosque. "Charleston did not have a tradition of houses of faith working together," Reverend Darby reflected. "But some kind of divine serendipity kicked in. All of those people who would normally say 'This is not going to work' came to the table." Since then, each year the ministry chooses one problem to tackle, proposes solutions, and addresses the issue at a large assembly where thousands of citizens come together with political and religious leaders. One of the justice ministry's first accomplishments was convincing the school board to expand early childhood education by funding hundreds of additional preschool slots. Then they lobbied successfully to reduce juvenile incarceration and school suspensions. They were already helping disadvantaged communities, but after the shooting, the ministry's focus turned to preventing racial profiling. "Before, they didn't talk about race," Reverend Darby told us. "But after the Emanuel tragedy a lightbulb went off in their heads. They realized they had to tackle race. It was fundamental to the challenges the community was facing."

We can work to prevent violence and racism but many forms of adversity can't be avoided. Loss. Accidental injury. Natural disasters. In 2010 alone, there were approximately four hundred natural disasters worldwide that claimed about 300,000 lives and affected millions. Some of the responses to these disasters show us that shared hope, experiences, and narratives can light the spark of collective resilience. But for the fire to be sustained we need shared power—the resources and authority to shape our own destiny.

Resilient communities have strong social ties—bonds between people, bridges between groups, and links to local leaders. I observed the importance of these local ties when I worked at the World Bank on leprosy eradication in India decades ago. Because of historic stigma, leprosy patients often fail to seek treatment, allowing their disease to progress and spread to others. When health workers visited villages to identify people with leprosy, they were rebuffed; the local people did not trust these outsiders, and women especially were reluctant to show spots on their skin to strangers. The health workers needed to find another approach. They convinced village leaders to run early detection programs themselves. The leaders held community meetings and recruited local nonprofits and citizens to perform plays showing that anyone coming forward with early symptoms would not be ostracized but would receive treatment and care.

This work made me acutely aware that even the most heroic examples of individual resilience can be inadequate in the face of poverty and untreated illness. When people with leprosy were kicked out of their villages, no amount of individual resilience could have helped them. It was not until the community began treating leprosy patients rather than banishing them that people could recover and survive.

Empowering communities builds collective resilience. After the 1994 genocide in Rwanda that killed hundreds of thousands of civilians, psychologists went to refugee camps in Tanzania to provide mental health care. They found that treating individuals was less effective than strengthening the community's ability to support vulnerable groups. The camps with the greatest resilience were organized like villages, with councils, meeting spaces for teenagers to hang out, soccer fields, entertainment venues, and places for worship. Instead of having outsiders in authority roles, the Rwandans led according to their cultural traditions. Self-organization provided order and built shared power.

Other times, collective resilience is needed to fight unjust cultural traditions. In China, women who are single past the age of twenty-seven are stigmatized as *sheng nu,* or "leftover women." They face severe pressure from their families to marry, stemming from the widespread belief that regardless of education and professional achievement, a woman is "absolutely nothing until she is married." One thirty-six-year-old economics professor was rejected by fifteen men because she had an advanced degree; her father then forbade her younger sister from going to graduate school. More than 80,000 women have joined Lean In Circles in China, and they are working together to build shared power. One of the Circles created *The Leftover Monologues,* a play where fifteen women and three men take back the term "leftover" while also speaking out against homophobia and date rape.

Just a few months after Dave died, I met with twenty Circle members from across China. In an effort to keep as many commitments as I could, I traveled to Beijing to speak at the Tsinghua University business school commencement, bringing my parents and children with me. It was the first time I had spoken publicly since becoming a widow and I was still in a fog. But spending time with these brave women right before the speech lifted my spirits. I had met with the same group two years earlier and was eager to hear about the progress they'd made. They talked about the compassion they felt for one another and for themselves. They spoke of changing careers and insisting to their parents that they were going to find their own life partners in their own time. And they spoke of action they were taking together that they never would have dared to take alone. I felt that tingling sensation in my chest and that lump in my throat. It was the best possible reminder that being part of a community can give us strength that we sometimes can't find on our own.

We find our humanity—our will to live and our ability to love—in our connections to one another. Just as individuals can find post-traumatic growth and become stronger, so can communities. You never know when your community will need to call on that strength, but you can be sure that someday it will.

When their plane crashed in the Andes, the rugby teammates had already built solidarity and trust. Early on they looked to the team captain for guidance. When he didn't make it, they maintained confidence in one another. "We all have our own personal Andes," Nando Parrado wrote long after the expedition with Roberto Canessa that led to their rescue. Canessa added, "One of the things that was destroyed when we crashed into the mountain was our connection to society. But our ties to one another grew stronger every day."

9

Failing and Learning
at Work

I N A YEAR FILLED WITH DESPAIR, one of the few high-
lights for me was watching a bunch of grown men cry.
There were women crying too, but I had seen that more
often.

It was April 2016 and I was close to crossing the finish line on
the Year of Firsts with three dreaded milestones still to go. My
son's first birthday without a father. My first wedding anniversary without a spouse. And a new unwelcome anniversary: the
first anniversary of Dave's death.

There were so many depressing firsts that I wanted to find
a positive one for my kids, so I took them to Los Angeles to
visit SpaceX's headquarters. After failing on four previous tries,
SpaceX was attempting to land a rocket at sea. Our invitation
came from Elon Musk, the company's CEO. The first time Elon
and I crossed paths after Dave died, he told me how sorry he
was and then added, "I understand how hard this is." In 2002,
Elon's first child died suddenly at two and a half months old.

We did not say much more and just sat together, bonded by grief.

On the day of the launch, my kids and I were on our feet along with a crowd of SpaceX employees in the company foyer. The countdown started on a large screen in front of us and the rocket in Florida took off on time. Everyone cheered. The rocket's steering arms opened as planned. More cheers. Each time there was a visible success, SpaceX employees would high-five the team that had worked on that component and then everyone would cheer together.

As the rocket approached the drone ship to attempt the ocean landing, the tension in the room grew. The cheering stopped and the crowd got very quiet. My heart was racing and my daughter and son grasped my hands nervously. My daughter whispered to me, "I hope it doesn't blow up!" I nodded, barely able to speak. As the rocket descended, three of the legs deployed but one lagged behind, tipping the rocket off target. The whole room leaned to one side as if trying to correct the position. Then the rocket tilted back and landed safely. The room erupted like a rock concert. Support crew, technicians, and engineers screamed and hugged and cried. My kids and I cried too. I still get chills thinking about it.

A few years ago, two management researchers became curious about what factors predict whether a space flight will succeed. Going back to the first launch of Sputnik 1 in 1957, they tracked every launch globally for nearly five decades across thirty organizations—mostly governments but also some private companies. You might think the best odds of a successful launch would come after past success, but the data from more than four thousand launches showed the exact opposite. The more times a government or company had failed, the more likely they were to put a rocket into orbit successfully on the next try. Also, their chances of success increased after a rocket exploded compared to a smaller failure. Not only do we learn more from failure than success, we learn more from bigger failures because we scrutinize them more closely.

Long before the water landing, the first time SpaceX attempted a launch, the engine caught fire thirty-three seconds after ignition and the rocket was destroyed. Elon had asked for the top ten risks in advance of the launch, and the problem that caused the failure turned out to be number eleven. *Pro tip: ask for top eleven risks.* The second launch failed for a relatively minor reason. The third launch would have succeeded if not for a tiny software bug. "I had basically assumed that we would have money for three attempts," Elon reflected. "When that third failure happened, I was just shredded." When my kids and I witnessed the successful water landing, the moment was even more meaningful because the triumph had followed so many disappointments.

Just as all people need resilience, all organizations do too. We see it in the companies that kept going after losing hundreds of employees on September 11. We see it in the businesses that rebound after financial crises and the nonprofits that regroup after losing donors. I saw it at the company Dave led, SurveyMonkey, when employees in the midst of grieving rallied around the hashtag #makedaveproud. When failures, mistakes, and tragedies happen, organizations make choices that affect the speed and strength of their recovery—and often determine whether they collapse or thrive.

To be resilient after failures, we have to learn from them. Most of the time, we know this; we just don't do it. We're too insecure to admit mistakes to ourselves or too proud to admit them to others. Instead of opening up, we get defensive and shut down. A resilient organization helps people overcome these reactions by creating a culture that encourages individuals to acknowledge their missteps and regrets.

Recently, this chalkboard was put up in the middle of New York City:

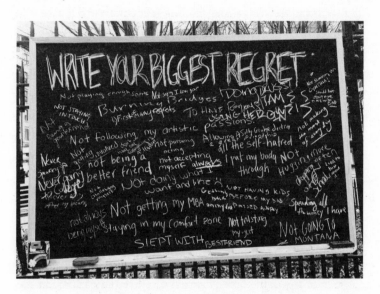

Of the hundreds of answers, most had one thing in common: the majority of regrets were about failures to act, not actions that failed. Psychologists have found that over time we usually regret the chances we missed, not the chances we took. As my mom often told me when I was growing up, "You regret the things you don't do, not the things you do."

At Facebook, we recognize that to encourage people to take risks, we have to embrace and learn from failure. When I joined the company, we had posters all over the walls that read, "Move fast and break things," and we meant it. In 2008, a summer intern named Ben Maurer was trying to stop our site from crashing. Hoping to debug the problem, he decided to trigger the failure himself and accidentally brought Facebook down for thirty minutes. In Silicon Valley, an outage is one of the biggest debacles a company can face, but instead of criticizing Ben, our lead engineer announced we should deliberately trigger failures more often—although preferably in ways that don't crash the site. He christened this practice "Ben Testing," and we hired Ben full-time.

Facebook is a relatively young company, so our management team goes on a yearly visit to an organization with staying power. We've been to Pixar, Samsung, Procter & Gamble, Walmart, and the Marine Corps Base Quantico. At Quantico, we went through basic training. To get a taste of the experience, we ran at night with our gear while officers shouted at us. The shouting continued as we performed smaller tasks like making beds and turning faucets on and off with military precision. The next day, in teams of four, we had to move heavy bags over a wall without letting them touch the ground. This was challenging for tech types, who are more used to loading digital documents than loading cargo; very few of our teams completed any of the tasks. I wasn't surprised that I failed at the physical challenges. What I didn't expect was that I would fail at following a command to *turn off a faucet*.

Before Quantico, I never would have run a full debrief after an obviously disastrous performance. When things went wrong at work, it was important to me that the people responsible for the mistake acknowledge it. But once they did, sitting down together to discuss in excruciating detail how and why the mistake was made just seemed like piling on. I also worried that this level of scrutiny might discourage risk taking. I was surprised that after every mission—and even after every training session—the Marines do formal debriefs. Then they record the lessons learned in a repository so that everyone can access them.

The Marines taught me the importance of creating a culture where failure is seen as a learning opportunity. When done insensitively, debriefs feel like public flagellation, but when expected and required, they no longer feel personal. In hospitals, where decisions have life and death consequences, healthcare professionals hold morbidity and mortality conferences. The purpose of "M&Ms" is to review the cases of patients where something went seriously wrong and figure out how to prevent similar problems in the future. The mistakes can range from a complication during surgery to an incorrect dose of a drug to a misdiagnosis of a disease. The discussions are confidential and evidence shows they can lead to improvements in patient care.

When it's safe to talk about mistakes, people are more likely to report errors and less likely to make them. Yet typical work cultures showcase successes and hide failures. Just look at any résumé; I have never seen one with a section called Things I Do Poorly. Scientist Melanie Stefan wrote an article challenging her peers to be more honest in their CVs. Princeton professor Johannes Haushofer took her up on it and posted his failure résumé—a list that went on for two pages of rejections from degree programs, job openings, academic journals, fellowships, and scholarships. He later noted, "This darn CV of failures has received way more attention than my entire body of academic work."

Convincing people to be more open about failure is not easy. Kim Malone Scott, who worked with me at Google, used to bring a stuffed monkey named Whoops to her team's weekly meetings. She would ask colleagues to share mistakes from that week and then they'd all vote for the biggest screwup. The "winner" got to keep the stuffed monkey on their desk where everyone could see it until the next week, when someone else earned the honor. Nothing could have been a better reminder to try hard things and discuss failures openly. Probably the only member of the team who didn't feel good about this exercise was Whoops, who never got a week off from being the symbol of imperfection.

Working with small businesses at Facebook has shown me that resilience is needed in organizations of all sizes. Damon Redd started the outdoor-clothing company Kind Design out of his basement in Colorado. When a flood filled his home with five feet of muddy water, he lost his designs, computers, and thousands of pieces of merchandise. He wasn't in a flood zone so he didn't have insurance to cover the loss. In an inventive effort to salvage damaged gloves, Damon power-washed and dried them, then started advertising them as "flood gloves." He posted about how the gloves and other products like hats, shirts, and hoodies symbolized the durability of the people of Colorado and his brand. His posts went viral and he racked up sales in all fifty states, saving his business.

Teams that focus on learning from failure outperform those that don't, but not everyone works in an organization that takes the long view. When that's the case, we can try to find our own ways to learn. When Adam was in graduate school, he was terrified of public speaking. After his first interview for a teaching job, he was told that he would never make it in the classroom because he wouldn't command enough respect from hard-nosed business school students. Professors are rarely taught how to teach, so to practice and improve, Adam volunteered to give guest lectures in other people's classes. These were tough audiences: instead of a whole semester to build relationships, he had only an hour to win over students. At the end of every guest lecture, Adam handed out feedback forms, asking how he could be more engaging and effective. The comments were not fun to read. Some students reported that Adam seemed so nervous that he made *them* physically shake in their seats.

After these sweat-soaked guest lectures, Adam started teaching his own class. A few weeks into the course, he asked the students to write anonymous feedback. Then he did something several colleagues called insane: he emailed the full set of comments to the entire class. Another professor warned Adam that doing this would be like dumping fuel on a fire. But one of Adam's colleagues, Sue Ashford, had taught him that gathering and acting on negative feedback is how you reach your potential. Sue's studies show that although fishing for compliments hurts your reputation, asking for criticism signals that you care about improving.

Adam opened the next class with an analysis of the major themes in his students' comments. Next, he shared how he would act on their feedback, like telling personal stories more often to bring concepts to life. Students were able to shape their own learning, and the class culture changed so that Adam was learning from them. A few years later, Adam became Wharton's top-rated professor. Each semester he continues to ask students for feedback, then shares their comments openly and makes changes to his teaching approach.

We all have blind spots—weaknesses that other people see but we don't. Sometimes we're in denial. Other times we simply don't know what we're doing wrong. The people who have taught me the most in my career are the ones who pointed out what I didn't see. At Google, my colleague Joan Braddi explained that I wasn't as persuasive as I could be in meetings because I often jumped in to speak early. She said that if I could be more patient and let others express their views first, I could make my arguments better by addressing their concerns. David Fischer, who runs our global teams at Facebook, often reminds me that I need to slow down and listen more.

Sometimes feedback is hard to take. About four months after I lost Dave, I got a call from his poker buddy Chamath Palihapitiya, who used to work with me at Facebook. Chamath said he was coming over to take me for a walk. So I put on my collar and started pacing around near my front door. (Okay, not quite, but I was excited to see him.) I expected Chamath to check in on how my daughter and son and I were doing, but he surprised me by saying that he wanted to make sure I was still pushing myself at work. I looked at him in shock—and admittedly some anger. "You want me to do more? Are you kidding me?" I explained that it was all I could do just to get through each day without messing up too much. Chamath rejected that completely; he said that I could yell at him all I wanted but he would always be there to remind me that I still needed to set ambitious goals. He advised me, as only Chamath could, "to get back on the motherf***ing path." Challenging someone like this could easily backfire, but Chamath knew me well enough to recognize that his blunt encouragement would provide a needed jolt of confidence—and remind me that I could fail by failing to try. He also inspired the only paragraph in this book that uses the f-word.

One of the best ways to see ourselves clearly is to ask others to hold up a mirror. "Top athletes and singers have coaches," surgeon and author Atul Gawande reflects. "Should you?" In basketball, Gregg Popovich has coached the San Antonio Spurs to five NBA championships. After losing in the finals one year, he sat down with the team to review every single play of the previous two games and learn what they did wrong. "The measure of who we are is how we react to something that doesn't go our way," he said. "There are always things you can do better. It's a game of mistakes."

Sports teams are recognizing the importance of looking for players who can learn from failure. In 2016, the Chicago Cubs won the World Series after a 108-year drought. General manager Theo Epstein explained why: "We will always spend more than half the time talking about the person rather than the player. . . . We would ask our scouts to provide three detailed examples of how these young players faced adversity on the field and responded to it, and three examples of how they faced adversity off the field. Because baseball is built on failure. The old expression is that even the best hitter fails seven out of ten times."

In sports, taking suggestions from a coach is the whole point of practice. Adam traces his openness to feedback to his past as a Junior Olympic diver. Criticism was the only way to get better. When it was time for Adam to enter the classroom, he ditched the Speedo but kept the strategy. He turned his students into his coaches.

Accepting feedback is easier when you don't take it personally. Being open to criticism means you get even more feedback, which makes you better. One way to lessen the sting of criticism is to evaluate how well you handle it. "After every low score you receive," law professors Doug Stone and Sheila Heen advise, you should "give yourself a 'second score' based on how you handle the first score. . . . Even when you get an F for the situation itself, you can still earn an A+ for how you deal with it."

The ability to listen to feedback is a sign of resilience, and some of those who do it best gained that strength in the hardest way possible. I met Byron Auguste when I was an associate at McKinsey and we were assigned to work on the same project. The first African American director in the company's history, Byron had a calmness that allowed him to see feedback as, in his words, "purely anthropological." He later told me that this attitude comes in part from the trauma he suffered as a teenager. When Byron was fifteen, he was walking to dinner with his cousin, younger brother, and dad near their home in Phoenix. Out of nowhere, a drunk driver plowed into the group,

breaking both of Byron's legs. When he woke up in the hospital, his mother had to tell him the horrible news that his father
was in a coma and his ten-year-old brother had died.

After the accident, Byron vowed not to become a problem for
his grieving parents. He excelled in school all the way through
earning a PhD in economics. What helped him build resilience
the most, he told me, was overcoming pervasiveness: "Extreme
compartmentalization may be my biggest superpower," he
said, laughing. If a project doesn't turn out the way he wanted,
Byron remembers that things could always be worse. "I say to
myself and to others all the time, 'Is anyone gonna die?' That's
the worst—I'm not afraid of failure."

Byron showed me that building resilient teams and organizations takes open and honest communication. When companies fail, it's usually for reasons that almost everyone knows
but almost no one has voiced. When someone isn't making
good decisions, few have the guts to tell that person, especially
if that person is the boss.

One of my favorite posters on our office walls reads, "Nothing at Facebook is someone else's problem." In a company-wide
meeting, I asked everyone facing challenges in working with a
colleague—which is of course everyone—to speak more hon-
estly to that person. I set a goal that we would all have at least
one hard conversation each month. To help the conversations
go well, I reminded everyone that feedback should always go
both ways. I talked about how a single sentence can make people more open to negative feedback: "I'm giving you these comments because I have very high expectations and I know that
you can reach them."

Now when I visit our offices around the world, I ask each
team: Who has had at least one hard conversation in the past
month? At first, very few hands went up. (And let's face it: when
I'm standing in front of them, my colleagues are more likely to

overreport than underreport.) As I've persisted, I've seen more and more hands go up and some of our leaders have taken bold steps to make openness to feedback part of our culture. Carolyn Everson, who runs our global sales teams, shares her performance reviews in an internal Facebook group with 2,400 members. She wants her entire team to see how she's working to improve.

As my Year of Firsts came to a close, I started thinking about one more hard conversation—a big one. Each year, I host a leadership day for women at Facebook. The previous year, I shared stories about my professional and personal fears and failures. I talked about times in my life that I felt truly unsure of who I was. I admitted to having made many bad decisions, including getting married and divorced in my early twenties and then going on to date a few wrong men. Then I talked about ending up in a true partnership with Dave. That year, my conclusion was: "Believing it will all work out helps it all work out."

A year later, I was in a very different place. I also had a heightened awareness that others in the room were struggling too. One coworker's mother was terminally ill. Another coworker was going through a difficult divorce. And those were just the two I knew about. I was sure that many were suffering in silence as we often do at work. I decided to open up in the hope that it might help others with hardships in their lives. I spoke about the three P's and what deep grief felt like. I admitted that I had not understood how hard it was to be a single parent or to stay focused at work when you're struggling at home. I was worried that I wouldn't get through the speech without crying . . . and I didn't. Still, by the end, I felt a sense of relief. In the weeks that followed, others at work started opening up as well. Together, we sent a bunch of elephants stampeding right out of our building.

One of the women in the room that day was Caryn

Marooney. I knew Caryn had a big decision to make since we had recently offered her a promotion to run our global communications team. But that decision had become far more complicated. Caryn's doctor had just told her that she might have breast cancer. She was waiting for test results but had already made up her mind that if her diagnosis was positive, she would not accept the promotion. "The combo of being afraid of failing in a new job and then being told you might have cancer was overwhelming," she told me. Caryn didn't feel comfortable discussing her medical issues at work; she didn't want to burden anyone and was afraid of appearing weak. But after hearing me open up about my struggles in front of thousands of coworkers, she saw a glimmer of possibility.

The next week Caryn's doctor confirmed that she had cancer and would require surgery and ongoing treatment. I asked her what she wanted to do about work and assured her that she had our full support no matter what she decided. She told me that meeting other patients made her realize how lucky she was that her cancer was caught at an early stage and that she worked for a company that gave her so much flexibility. She said she was scared but did not want to give up a role she'd been working toward for so many years. Together, we laid out a plan for her to take the new job.

"I had to jettison the notion of being a 'fearless leader,'" Caryn said. Instead, the first time she addressed the two-hundred-person global communications team, she spoke openly about her diagnosis. She was undergoing daily radiation treatments, which were physically draining and made her forgetful. "In any version of picturing this moment—that fantasy of what you want to be—I would have been strong, smart, and inspiring confidence," she told me. "I wanted to be a role model in that perfect 'put together' sense. Instead, I told them I had cancer and would need *their* support."

Their response blew her away. Caryn's teammates pulled together to help—and started sharing more of their own personal and professional challenges. Caryn believes that this openness made their work more efficient. "You'd think sharing would slow you down, but it takes time and energy to hide things," Caryn said. Being more open personally led people to be more open professionally. Caryn's team used to discuss "lessons learned" in one-on-one meetings, but most people were not comfortable discussing failure in larger groups. "Lessons learned" is now something that the full team has embraced. "Before, we used to talk about what went well," Caryn said. "Now, we cover what went wrong too."

Caryn powered through her own Year of Firsts. She has led the global communications team *and* made it through radiation. On her first day of treatment, I gave her a necklace with the letters "YGT." She was confused at first since her initials are "CLM." I explained that it was a symbol of my faith in her and stood for "You've got this."

"I now say 'YGT' to my team all the time," Caryn said. "And they say it to each other. YGT. It means so much."

10

To Love and Laugh Again

A T THE TIME OF OUR WEDDING in 2004, Dave was
working at Yahoo and I was working at Google. We
thought one way of handling the rivalry between our
companies—and some of our wedding guests—was to make a
joke of it by giving everyone a choice of baseball hats. It would
be our version of "Are you with the bride or the groom?" I
ordered the Google hats way in advance and was feeling pretty
good about them until Dave took one of my hats to the Yahoo
office and said, "Make ours nicer." They did, and to the delight
of the Yahoo team, many of the Google guests wore Yahoo hats
all weekend.

Love and laughter were always intertwined for Dave and
me, and we wanted our wedding to reflect that. At my bridal
brunch, I gave all my girlfriends a Mr. Wonderful doll. When
you squeezed the doll's hand, it spoke, saying things like
"Let's just cuddle tonight" or "Aw, can't your mother stay
another week?" My favorite was "You take the remote. As
long as I'm with you, I don't care what we watch." At our
rehearsal dinner, my brother-in-law Marc took humor to a
whole new level, narrating a slide show of me and my past

boyfriends. And yes, the phrase "dude with a nipple ring" did come up.

Our wedding took place on a beautiful and extremely breezy Arizona day. Right before the ceremony, Dave and I gathered in a small room with our family and closest friends to sign the vows we'd written as part of our *ketubah,* the Jewish wedding contract. I signed first then Dave added his bold, messy signature. We headed outdoors, where an aisle had been laid on an open lawn. The procession began, and just as I stepped into place I heard Marc ahead of me egging on our three-year-old ring bearer: "Hey, Jasper, I've heard this wedding is pants optional." My sister jumped in: "Jasper, no more spit bombs!" I started down the makeshift aisle, still laughing from the Jasper exchange, when a gust of wind blew my veil so far up in the air that I almost fell over. I stabilized, joined Dave, and the rabbi began.

Traditionally, a Jewish bride circles her groom seven times. Dave and I circled each other, our eyes locked. Our friends said it looked like we were dancing. Then, surrounded by our parents and siblings, we faced each other and paragraph by paragraph recited the vows we'd written together:

I take you to be mine in love. I promise to love you deliberately each day, to feel your joy and your sorrow as my own. Together, we will build a home filled with honor and honesty, comfort and compassion, learning and love.

I take you to be mine in friendship. I vow to celebrate all that you are, to help you become the person you aspire to be. From this day forward, your dreams are my dreams and I dedicate myself to helping you fulfill the promise of your life.

I take you to be mine in faith. I believe that our commitment to each other will last a lifetime, that with you, my soul is complete.

Knowing who I am and who I want to be, on this day of our marriage, I give you my heart to be forever united with yours.

We spent eleven years living these vows, circling each other in love and friendship. Then, suddenly, Dave's forever was over. Each night, my brokenhearted march to bed included seeing our vows as I walked past our *ketubah* hanging on the bedroom wall near Dave's closet. The sight of both pained me, especially his clothes, which hung there as if waiting for him to come home—as I was.

After several months, I was still holding my breath as I walked past this wall and realized that I needed to do something. I could not bear to take our *ketubah* down—it hangs there still—so I decided to clean out Dave's closet. It's impossible to describe how much I dreaded this task. Nothing prepares you for this. Carole Geithner advised me to include my son and daughter, and the three of us started together. We laughed—which shocked me—at the pile of almost identical gray sweaters and shirts from conferences that Dave had attended decades before. We cried when we pulled out his beloved Vikings jersey. My kids selected what they wanted to keep, and as my daughter hugged one of his sweaters she blurted out what we'd all been thinking: "The clothes smell like Daddy."

Later that night, Dave's mother Paula and his brother Rob came upstairs to help me finish. They had already performed this miserable task once when they cleaned out Dave's father's closet sixteen years earlier. They never thought they would be doing this for Dave, and the completely surreal feeling overwhelmed all three of us. Paula held up the frayed gray sweater Dave wore most often and I broke down completely. I turned to her and said, "I can't believe you are going through this *again*. How are you okay? How can you *possibly* be okay?" She said, "I didn't die. Mel did and Dave did, but I am alive. And I am going to live." She put her arm around me and said, "And you are going to live too." Then she completely stunned me by adding, "And you are not only going to live, but you are going to get remarried one day—and I am going to be there to celebrate with you."

Until then, I had not thought about finding love again. Months earlier, I had mentioned to Rob that I was going to take down the photograph of a beach at night that hung in my bedroom. Dave and I had selected the photograph together but now its dark imagery felt too depressing. I told Rob I wanted to replace it with a picture of me, Dave, and our kids. Rob shook his head. "This is your bedroom," he said. "No pictures of Dave. You're going to move on."

Moving on is easier said than done. I couldn't bear to take off my wedding ring, but every time I saw it on my left hand I felt I was living in denial. I moved the ring to my right hand so I could still feel connected to Dave but wasn't pretending that I was still married. Since I couldn't even sort out my feelings for an inanimate object, I really couldn't bring myself to consider the possibility of dating, let alone talk about it. It felt disloyal and just reminded me how much I wanted Dave back. So when Rob implied that there might be someone else in my life one day, I quickly changed the subject.

At the same time, I had never wanted to be alone. My parents have a very loving marriage, and since childhood I longed to have one too. I think that this led me to get married too young the first time. I know that a stronger sense of independence and the confidence that I could take care of myself would have helped me throughout my dating life. After my first marriage ended in divorce, I had a repetitive stress dream where I would wake up looking for someone who was supposed to be sleeping next to me, see the empty bed, and realize that I was alone. After I married Dave, the dream still happened, but then I would wake up to see him next to me—or more frequently hear him snoring next to me—and feel that oh-I-was-just-dreaming relief.

Now the stress dream was real. I was alone in my bed. Alone when my kids went on playdates. Just one hour in my house without them made me project into the future to when they would go off to college, leaving me behind. Would I be alone for the rest of my life?

Marne reminded me that being alone can be an empowering choice. In a landmark fifteen-year study of changes in marital status among more than 24,000 people, getting married increased average happiness only a little bit; on a scale of 0 to 10, single people who were at a 6.7 in happiness might increase to a 6.8 after getting married. That tiny boost occurred around the time of the wedding and typically faded within a year. If one of the participants lost a spouse and did not remarry, eight years later on average their happiness would be a 6.55. It turns out that people who choose to be single are very satisfied with their lives. "Singles are stereotyped, stigmatized, and ignored," psychologist Bella DePaulo finds, "and still live happily ever after." She asks us to imagine a world where married people are treated like singles: "When you tell people you are married, they tilt their heads and say things like 'Aaaawww' or 'Don't worry, honey, your turn to divorce will come.' . . . At work, the single people just assume that you can cover the holidays and all the other inconvenient assignments."

Like all couples, Dave and I had moments when we were out of sync, but we always tried to address the issue head-on. One thing we never addressed was the situation I now found myself in. I had told Dave that if I died, I wanted him to find love again—as long as he did not marry a woman who would be an evil stepmother and force our children to wear coats made from Dalmatians. Dave said it was an awful conversation and never shared a single wish with me. Now I encourage my friends and family to express their fears and desires to their partners.

Love is the third rail of grief—a topic so charged that it is untouchable. After losing a partner, the only thing more emotionally fraught than finding joy is finding love. The mere thought of dating someone else triggers sadness followed by guilt. If just dancing with a childhood friend could make me burst into tears, imagine . . .

How soon is too soon to date? I heard about a woman in England who lost her husband and began dating his best friend four weeks later. People were shocked at how quickly her new romance started. Her mother-in-law cut off communication with her and many of her friends did too. "Blame me if you like," the woman said, "but grief hits people in different ways and I have no regrets." When you are widowed, people pity you and want your sorrow to end. But if you start dating, sometimes they judge you and think maybe your sorrow ended just a wee bit too soon. A childhood friend of mine who is now a rabbi told me that in the Jewish religion, mourning for a parent, child, or sibling is a year, but mourning for a spouse is just thirty days. "The rabbis wanted people to move forward," he said.

About four months into my widowhood, my brother David said there was something he wanted to talk to me about. "I don't know if it's okay to mention this," he said, sounding much more hesitant than he usually does, "but I think you should start thinking about dating." Like Rob, he assured me that Dave would never have wanted me to be alone. David believed it would help distract me and make me feel better about my future. He also pointed out that if I were a man, I would have started dating already.

Sure enough, after a partner dies, men are more likely to date than women and they start dating sooner. Of middle-aged adults

who lost a spouse, 54 percent of men were in a romantic relationship a year later, compared with only 7 percent of women.
In the U.K., men were approximately twice as likely as women
to have remarried within five years of the loss of a spouse. And
in India, the majority of men remarried after losing a spouse,
compared with only ten percent of women. Men who start new
relationships are judged less harshly. Women are expected to
carry the torch of love, and when that flame is extinguished
they are supposed to mourn for it longer. The weeping widow
lives up to our expectations. The widow who dances and dates
does not. These differences reflect a double standard rooted
in a range of issues, from women feeling more guilt and anxiety about new romances to a greater cultural acceptance of
men marrying younger women to the demographic reality
of women living longer than men.

One practical matter that falls more heavily on women is
the responsibility to care for children and aging parents. A
colleague of mine told me about her extended family, which
includes four single moms, and not one ever dated let alone
remarried. "I'm sure there are lots of reasons," she said. "But
the one that they would all point to was that they didn't have
the time or the money to date while raising their children."
Most of her relatives had to work multiple jobs to support their
families since the men didn't pay child support. The women
absolutely wanted to find romantic love again, but it took all
of their strength just to keep a roof over their children's heads.
They couldn't afford babysitters and lived far from family or
friends who could have pitched in to help. For them, dating was
a luxury they could not afford.

Widows continue to face cruel treatment around the world.
In some parts of India, widows are cast away by their own families, left to beg to survive. In some Nigerian villages, widows
are stripped naked and forced to drink water that has been used

to bathe their dead husbands. Discrimination against widows has been observed by 54 percent of people in China, 70 percent in Turkey, and 81 percent in South Korea. In many countries, widows have difficulty obtaining property rights.

Since there are few things that motivate me more than telling me that something is sexist, after my brother spoke up I started thinking about dating. As I tried to wrap my head around it, the questions swirled: Would trying to move on just make it all worse? Would dating be as dreadful as it had been before? I started occasionally writing about dating in my journals. But when I shared entries with my closest friends and family—which I did when it was easier than talking about my feelings—I edited these parts out. I felt guilty even thinking about it and worried about their reactions.

Several months later, I told Phil that I'd been emailing with a friend and it was starting to feel almost flirty. Phil's initial reaction confirmed my fears: "I am your friend always," he said, "but Dave was my close friend. I'm not ready for this." Phil's aunt, who had lost her husband a year earlier, was with us. Later that day when they were alone, Phil told her that he thought he had done "a pretty good job at handling an awkward conversation." His aunt replied, "You were awful."

Phil was taken aback. At first, he defended his position, explaining to her, "I was following the guy code. I was trying to respect Dave, not judge Sheryl." But his aunt told him that even if he hadn't meant any offense, his response was not supportive. Phil came back to my house and apologized. He added that he hoped we could talk about anything, including dating. We hugged and he said wistfully, "I guess we both need to move on."

Others were less accepting. When the press reported that I was seeing someone, one man posted that I was a "garbage whore." Another quipped that clearly I was "one classy lady"

because the love of my life died and I was "already sharing flu-
ids with a new guy."

Fortunately, we can also find understanding on the internet.
I read a blog by author Abel Keogh about trying to date after his
wife died by suicide. He wrote, "The first time I went to dinner with another woman, I felt like I was cheating on my late
wife. . . . I was filled with feelings of guilt and betrayal." After
six months, he met a woman at church. On their first date, he
told her he was a widower; she was put off and did not want to
see him again. Her father encouraged her to give him a second
chance. Less than a year later they married. They now have
seven children and Abel has written dating guides for widowers. "There will always be someone who will not understand
why you've chosen to date again," he lamented. "They may
give you a hard time or have some silly notion that widows and
widowers shouldn't fall in love again. Their opinions do not
matter. All that matters is that you're ready to date again. You
don't need to justify your actions."

People who have lost a spouse feel enough grief and guilt
on their own. Judging them makes those feelings worse. It's
kinder to see dating not as a betrayal but as an attempt for them
to break through the sorrow and find some joy. I'll always be
grateful that Paula, Rob, and David raised the subject. They
brought up the dating elephant and then escorted it politely out
of the room.

Still, dating does not erase my grief. All of us in the club
understand this. You can miss your spouse and be with someone else, especially if that person is secure enough to let you
grieve and help you through it. I had breakfast with a friend
three months after he lost his wife and said he should start
dating when he was ready, hoping to give him the same kind
encouragement that Dave's family had given me. Later, he
went on his first date and emailed me: "It was weird. And I

was still just as sad the next day. But as awkward as it was at moments, it felt like one of the first steps forward I have taken. I felt alive again."

I met Tracy Robinson this past summer when our kids attended the same camp. Like me, she was a widow with two children. For years, she felt deeply lonely without her husband Dan. She clung to her friends, becoming closer to some while others let her down. She was not thinking about dating—and then she met Michelle. "There's a kindness in her," she told me. "I love her in a very different way than I loved Dan." Tracy and Michelle married this past summer, five years after Dan died. Tracy still misses him and says that getting remarried has not changed that, but she feels strongly about seizing opportunities because life truly can be over in a heartbeat. "I almost hate to say this, but I am the happiest I have ever been in my life," she told me. "Sometimes it takes going through something so awful to realize the beauty that is out there in this world."

Brain scans of people in love reveal an intoxicating state of energy and euphoria. After we fall in love, we gain confidence and self-esteem and expand our identities. Often we take on some of our new partner's qualities; falling for someone who is curious or calm can make us see ourselves a bit more that way too.

Dating brought humor back into my life. The man I mentioned to Phil began emailing—at first intermittently and then more frequently—and in months and months of notes, he never failed to make me laugh. He called himself the "King of Distraction" and he was. He helped me focus more on the present and future and find moments of joy.

If love is the third rail of grief, laughter is equally charged. In the face of death, it feels wildly inappropriate to joke about anything. Even worse is joking about death itself. But every so often, I found myself doing it—and was then completely aghast, as if I had caught myself putting my hand *and arm* into some forbidden cookie jar. The first joke I remember making was when an ex-boyfriend walked into my house after the funeral. He hugged me and said how sorry he was. "This is all your fault," I responded. "If you had been straight, we would have gotten married and then none of this would have happened." We both laughed. And then I gasped, horrified at myself for making the joke.

A few weeks later, my sister-in-law Amy and I were upstairs in my room, crying together. I looked up and said, "Well, at least I don't have to watch his bad movies anymore." We were both stunned into silence. Then we burst into laughter because Dave really did have terrible taste in movies—almost as bad as my taste in TV shows. I still cringe every time I think of these jokes, but they pushed away the overwhelming darkness of the moment. Later, Rob did the same thing, blurting out that he would never forgive his brother for leaving him with a mother, wife, and sister-in-law who were all calling him twenty times a day. It was funny because it was true. And unfortunately for Rob, I didn't take the hint and call him any less often.

The gasping has faded and now I can make jokes about Dave quite easily, as long as they are the same jokes we made together when he was alive. Jokes about *his death*, however, are still shockers. But they do help break the tension. One day a friend of ours who knew that Dave wanted our son to go to private school noted with surprise that he is attending a public middle school. I said, "If Dave wanted our children to go to private school, he should have stuck around to make it happen." Our friend froze for a second and then relaxed as it dawned on him that I was joking. We then had our first real conversation since Dave died.

Humor can make us more resilient. Surgery patients who watch comedies request 25 percent less pain medication. Soldiers who make jokes deal better with stress. People who laugh naturally six months after losing a spouse cope better. Couples who laugh together are more likely to stay married. Physiologically, humor lowers our heart rate and relaxes our muscles. Evolutionarily, humor is a signal that a situation is safe. Laughter breaks tension by making stressful situations less threatening.

Humor can also provide a little dash of morality in which wrongs are righted. When you take a horrible situation and add a punch line to it, for at least a moment you have shifted the balance of power: the helpless become the victors and the underdog gets the last word. Mel Brooks said he made fun of Hitler and the Nazis because "if you can reduce them to ridicule then you're way ahead." For centuries, jesters were the only people who could speak truth to power and had permission to challenge a king or queen. Today in the United States, late-night TV comedians play this role.

Jokes are common at funerals because gallows humor helps us triumph over sadness. Before writing *Lean In* with me, Nell Scovell wrote for TV comedies. She has four siblings, and when they lost their mom, she opened her eulogy by holding up an envelope and declaring, "I have in this envelope the name of Mom's favorite child." After one of Nell's friends was widowed, she started keeping a journal where she expressed her feelings to her deceased husband and noted, "He's a way better listener now." Comedian Janice Messitte's husband died suddenly two weeks after they got married. When she was asked how she lost her husband, she retorted, "He's not lost. He had a great sense of direction. He's DEAD." Humor can provide relief—even for a split second.

Trying to move on, I brought the King of Distraction to my cousin's wedding. It was a relief to have someone to dance with again, but being at a family wedding without Dave was still hard. I put on my game face as the music started playing. A woman came over and said, "I heard you were dating! I am so glad you're okay now!" Another woman shook hands with my date and then turned to me and exclaimed, "It's so nice to see you're over Dave's death!" I know they meant well and wanted me to be happy, but no, I am not "over" Dave's death. I never will be.

When we marry, we promise to love "till death do us part." Our images of love are active—we love by being there for a friend, taking care of a child, waking up next to someone—all of which depend upon the person being *alive*. One of the most important things I've learned is how deeply you can keep loving someone after they die. You may not be able to hold them or talk to them, and you may even date or love someone else, but you can still love them every bit as much. Playwright Robert Woodruff Anderson captured it perfectly: "Death ends a life, but it does not end a relationship."

Last summer, I had dinner with three couples who are all close friends of mine but were just getting to know one another. They went around the table sharing their stories of how they met, spouses interjecting the funny asides of a well-honed routine. As the conversation began, I got that feeling in the pit of my stomach, and as the conversation continued that feeling grew and grew. *Elephant, I never thought I'd miss you.* At first, I thought I was sad because it was insensitive of my friends to tell their love stories with me sitting right there. It had been fifteen months and three days since Dave's death, and for most people it was no longer at the forefront of their minds. The world had moved on. I went home early that night, explaining that I didn't feel well.

But the next morning, I woke up even more upset—not at my friends, who would never want to hurt me, but at the realization that no one would ever ask me again how Dave and I met. As the couples went around the table, they had skipped me. Now that Dave was gone, our cute how-we-met story was no longer cute. Asking people how they met their deceased partner seems cruel so no one does it. But for the widow or widower, not asking means they miss out on the nostalgia of recalling those early romantic days. I called Tracy Robinson and we agreed that from now on, we would both ask the members of our club how they met their partner to give them a chance to remember the excitement of that first encounter.

As Adam and I studied resilience at home and at work, we also thought about how to apply these lessons to relationships. We all want to forge bonds that can withstand stress, make both people stronger, and get us through life's ups and downs. In a new romance, it often seems easy. Psychologists find that when people are falling in love, even arguments make them more attracted to each other. *Ever heard of makeup sex?* Then people move out of the honeymoon phase and just dealing with the ordinary hassles of life can create strain. Sometimes adversity strikes without warning—a partner gets sick or laid off or depressed. Other times adversity stems from a mistake or bad choice—a partner cheats or lies or becomes unkind or abusive. Try as we might, sometimes relationships don't or shouldn't last.

To build resilience in a loving, long-term relationship, we need to pay attention to the everyday interactions we have with our partners. In a well-known study, 130 newlyweds were invited to spend the day at the "Love Lab," which resembled a bed-and-breakfast. The psychologists observed the couples interacting "in the wild" and made predictions about which marriages would last. They were able to predict divorce over the next six years with 83 percent accuracy. A key was buried in the couples' conversations, which often started with bids for attention, affection, support, or laughter. We are making a bid whenever we say things like "Hey, look at that bird!" or

"Are we out of butter?" When a partner makes a bid, the other partner has two choices: to turn away or turn toward. Turning away means dismissing or ignoring the bid. *Stop talking about birds, I'm watching TV.* Turning toward means engaging. *Yep, I'll go get some butter. And some popcorn to go with it.* The newlyweds who stayed together over the next six years turned toward each other 86 percent of the time, while couples who got divorced turned toward each other only 33 percent. Most of the couples' fights weren't about money or sex but about "failed bids for connection."

Adam's colleague Jane Dutton defines a resilient relationship as one that has the capacity to carry intense emotions and withstand strain. It's more than two resilient individuals connecting—resilience becomes a feature of the connection itself. My late friend Harriet Braiker was a therapist who published many books on love. She often said there were three parties in any relationship: you, the other person, and the relationship itself. The relationship is a meaningful entity that needs to be protected and nurtured.

Part of protecting and nurturing a bond is doing small things together. After falling in love, couples often find that the sparks fade, and one way to reignite them is to try new or exciting activities. I remember going to an out-of-town wedding where Dave and I spent most of the weekend playing Scrabble. A friend who was recently divorced watched us and remarked that he and his ex-wife never really did anything together—and that his new goal was to find someone who would play Scrabble with him. Apparently Scrabble was his idea of an exciting experience. Mine too.

For a relationship to last, partners have to be able to deal with conflict. When newlyweds were asked to talk for fifteen minutes about an ongoing disagreement in their marriage, the amount of anger expressed by a husband or wife had no bearing on whether the couple got divorced over the next six years. The most common pattern for couples that divorced went like this: the wife would bring up an issue, the husband would get belligerent or defensive, and then the wife would reciprocate with sadness, disgust, or stonewalling. In the couples whose marriages lasted, instead of escalating negativity, both partners showed humor and affection. They took responsibility for their problems and found ways to compromise. They sent signals that even though they were fighting, at a deeper level, they were okay.

When we argue with our partners, it's easy to get stuck in our own point of view. Taking a broader perspective helps resolve conflict. In one study, couples were instructed to write about their biggest disagreement as if they were outsiders looking in on the fight. Just three journal entries of seven minutes each were enough to help the couples maintain a loving marriage over the next year.

Of course, a strong relationship doesn't solve all problems. My friend Jennifer Joffe loves her husband and he loves her. They have two great kids. Jennifer is one of the kindest people I know, but for thirty-five years she was not kind to herself. "I disliked myself so much, hated myself truthfully, that I had no regard for my body," she said. Jennifer's father died when she was the same age as my daughter and that profound sadness triggered decades of compulsive eating. "I used food to medicate the pain of losing my dad," she said. "But as I got older I also used it to keep a protective layer between me and the world."

Then a few years ago, Jennifer's daughter was riding her bike home from school and got hit by a car. She was released from the hospital later that day but this near catastrophe jolted Jennifer's perspective. "When my biggest fear almost came true, I realized I was not really living my life," she said. She was able to stop her compulsive eating for a while, but by spring she was bingeing again. Then Dave died. Jennifer came over right away to comfort us. And in a beautiful twist, helping us turned out to help her too. "Just watching it all again was like being a ghost from Christmas past," she told me. "I looked at your daughter and wanted her to know her world had changed forever, and it was so unfair, but it wasn't her fault. It wasn't anyone's fault. It was just life. I wanted her to love herself. And I wanted my daughter to love herself. But how could I expect her—and my son—to do that when their own mother did not?"

At last, Jennifer started treating herself with the kindness and care she showed others. Her big breakthrough came when she realized "you cannot outrun any addiction. You must heal, and that takes a kind of love that no one else can provide for you." Once Jennifer found self-compassion and self-acceptance, she was able to gain control over her addiction and now coaches other women who struggle with emotional eating. She is a role model for me and a reminder that the love we need to lead a fulfilling life cannot only come from others but must come from inside us as well.

Like so much else in life, finding someone to love is not something we can control. As my Facebook colleague Nina Choudhuri got older, she grappled with her lifelong desire to get married and have children. Her parents had an arranged marriage, fell deeply in love, and then her father passed away when she was three. "The only reality I have known is growing up with a single mother who was not one by choice—that was her Option B," Nina says. Nina dreamed of getting married and starting a family. Her mother encouraged her to look for the right partner and marry for love. Nina started searching for the perfect man. In her twenties, she would go on a first date and immediately ask herself, "Is this someone I could marry?" Nina remained optimistic, but as more and more online matches and blind dates didn't pan out, she began to wonder if the dream she shared with her mother might not come true.

As Nina approached forty, she realized that she couldn't control whether she fell in love, but she could choose to have a child. She was worried about the risks of pregnancy, so she started thinking about adoption. "At forty-three, I had this aha moment of acceptance and realizing life is not about image—it's about fulfillment," she said. She decided to adopt a baby on her own. When she told her brother, he cheered and wrapped his arms around her. Her mom was ecstatic too, telling her a child is a gift from God. "All of this support further validates my feeling of 'Yes, I can do this!' I am lucky to be surrounded by so much love and care," Nina told me. "Who's to say that a family is a man, a woman, and two and a half children and a white picket fence? In my Option B, the B stands for 'baby.' The two of us together will create our Option A."

The process has required perseverance. Nina was selected by one birth mother, but the baby was born with a congenital heart defect and survived only a week. Nina told me at the time that she had no regrets. She said she "loved the baby for seven gorgeous days," and although it was a brutal experience, it reaffirmed her decision to adopt. Then just before Valentine's Day, Nina sent me an email with the subject line "Introducing . . ." My heart started beating faster when I saw a picture of her cradling a newborn just hours after birth. You can't see Nina's eyes in the photo because they are glued to her daughter. Her email contained this simple six-word message: "So in love! Can't believe it!"

Resilience in love means finding strength from within that you can share with others. Finding a way to make love last through the highs and lows. Finding your own way to love when life does not work out as planned. Finding the hope to love and laugh again when love is cruelly taken from you. And finding a way to hang on to love even when the person you love is gone.

———

As I write this, it has been almost two years since that unimaginable day in Mexico. Two years since my children lost their father. Two years since I lost the love of my life.

Anna Quindlen told me that we confuse resilience with closure. She lost her mother forty years ago. "Is it easier than it was then? Yes," she said to me over coffee. "Do I still miss her so much it feels like a toothache? Yes. Do I still pick up the phone and try to call her? Yes."

Time has marched on and in some ways, I have too. In other ways, I haven't. I now believe what Davis Guggenheim told me that first month: grief has to unfold. Writing this book and trying to find meaning have not replaced my sadness. Sometimes grief hits me like a wave, crashing into my consciousness until I can feel nothing else. It strikes at predictable big events, like our anniversary, and at the smallest of moments, like when junk mail comes to the house addressed to Dave. Sometimes I'll be working at my kitchen table and my heart will skip a beat when I think for a brief second that he is opening the door and coming home.

But just as grief crashes into us like a wave, it also rolls back like the tide. We are left not just standing, but in some ways stronger. Option B still gives us options. We can still love . . . and we can still find joy.

I now know that it's possible not just to bounce back but to grow. Would I trade this growth to have Dave back? *Of course.* No one would ever choose to grow this way. But it happens—

and we do. As Allen Rucker wrote about his paralysis, "I won't make your skin crawl by saying it's a 'blessing in disguise.' It's not a blessing and there is no disguise. But there are things to be gained and things to be lost, and on certain days, I'm not sure that the gains are not as great as, or even greater than, the inevitable losses."

Tragedy does not have to be personal, pervasive, or permanent, but resilience can be. We can build it and carry it with us throughout our lives. If Malala can feel gratitude . . . if Catherine Hoke can get her second chance to help others get a second chance . . . if "leftover" women can band together to fight social stigma . . . if the Mother Emanuel congregants can rise above hate . . . if Allen Rucker can keep his sense of humor . . . if Wafaa can flee to a strange country and rediscover joy . . . if Joe Kasper can forge a co-destiny with his son . . . we can all find strength within ourselves and build strength together. There is light within each of us that will not be extinguished.

At Dave's funeral, I said that if on the day I walked down the aisle with him, someone had told me that we would have only eleven years together, I would still have walked down that aisle. Eleven years of being Dave's wife and ten years of being a parent with him is perhaps more luck and more happiness than I could ever have imagined. I am grateful for every minute we had. I concluded my eulogy with these words:

Dave, I have a few promises I make to you today:

I promise I will raise your children as Vikings fans even though I know nothing about football and I'm pretty sure that team never wins.

I promise to take them to Warriors games and pay attention enough to cheer only when the Warriors score.

I promise to let our son continue to play online poker even though you let him start at eight years old and most fathers would have discussed with the mother whether it was appropriate for such a young child to play online poker in the first place. And to our daughter: when you are eight—but not one minute before—you can play online poker too.

Dave, I promise to raise your children so that they know who you were—and everyone here can help me do that by sharing your stories with us. And Dave, I will raise your children so that they know what you wanted for them and that you loved them more than anything in the world.

Dave, I promise to try to live a life that would make you proud. A life of doing my best, being the friend you were to our friends, following your example in trying to make the world a better place, and always—but always—cherishing your memory and loving our family.

Today we will put the love of my life to rest, but we will bury only his body. His spirit, his soul, his amazing ability to give is still with all of us. I feel it in the stories people are sharing of how he touched their lives, I see it in the eyes of our family and friends, and above all, it is in the spirit and resilience of our children. Things will never be the same—but the world is better for the years Dave Goldberg lived.

Yes, the world is better for the years Dave Goldberg lived. I am better for the years we spent together and for what he taught me—both in life and in death.

Building Resilience Together

We invite you to visit optionb.org to connect with others who are coping with challenges like yours. You can read stories of people who have built resilience in the face of loss, illness, abuse, and other adversity—and find information that will help you and your loved ones.

We also hope you'll join the Option B community at facebook.com/OptionBOrg for ongoing encouragement.

By coming together and supporting one another, we can bounce forward and find joy again.

Acknowledgments

When you're writing a book about resilience, people naturally start opening up about hardships that they or their loved ones have faced. Many of us had already worked together, but we all grew closer during this project. We appreciate everyone included here for their expertise and contributions and even more for their candor and trust.

Nell Scovell edited this book with heroic persistence. She thought carefully about every sentence and every paragraph with an unflagging dedication to getting it right. Nell has a remarkable set of skills and this book reflects them all. As a journalist, she is the master of shaping and honing stories. As a speechwriter, she has a deep understanding of how to capture voice. As a comedy writer, she provided much-needed humor, both on and off the page. We admire her attention to detail, her ability to get to the heart of each moment, and the real sacrifices that she made for this project out of loyalty and love. Her proficiency comes through on every page, and we could not have written this book without her.

Journalist Stacey Kalish conducted more than forty interviews, asking difficult questions with empathy. Stanford sociologist Marianne Cooper's sharp analysis focused our thinking, and her deep knowledge about social and economic inequality provided invaluable insight.

Our editor at Knopf, Robin Desser, understood the need to balance emotion and research and how to integrate the two. Her enthusiasm out of the gate helped us get to the finish line. Knopf's editor in chief Sonny Mehta and president Tony Chirico were our Option A and we are grateful for their support. We also thank CEO Markus Dohle for championing all of our work at Penguin Random House. Our agents Jennifer Walsh and Richard Pine gave exceptional counsel and friendship throughout every step of the process.

David Dreyer and Eric London are virtuosos of communication and trusted advisors whose steady voices of reason were a constant beacon. Liz Bourgeois and Anne Kornblut could not have been more generous with their time or more brilliant with their observations on people, tone, and emotion. Lachlan Mackenzie contributed his compassion and his unique gift for using imagery to illustrate difficult concepts. Gene Sperling came through time and time again with his knack for seeing around corners and solving problems we did not even realize we had. Merrill Markoe shined a light in the darkness and made us laugh out loud.

As the president of the Sheryl Sandberg & Dave Goldberg Family Foundation, Rachel Thomas has led LeanIn.Org's efforts to support women all over the world in pursuing their ambitions. Now she is expanding her focus to launch OptionB.Org. There is no one better at what she does. A huge thank-you to the entire team for the passion and creativity they bring to their work every day. Special kudos to Jenna Bott for her design talent, Ashley Finch for her leadership and execution, Katie Miserany and Sarah Maisel for helping people share their stories, Raena Saddler and Michael Linares for creating the Option B website, Megan Rooney and Brigit Helgen for always knowing what to say, Bobbi Thomason for localizing each edition, and Clarice Cho and especially Abby Speight for supporting the Option B community. Our heartfelt thanks to Norman Jean Roy for dedicating his immense talent to capturing the spirit of resilience in photos and to Dyllan McGee and her team at McGee Media for giving our heroes voice on film.

We were lucky to have advice and input from knowledgeable friends. Carole Geithner provided insight on how to help children through grief. Maxine Williams contributed her deep knowledge of bias and diversity. Marc Bodnick pushed us to find the right examples to illuminate the three P's. Amy Schefler taught us how hospitals learn from and prevent errors. Andrea Saul shared her communications and political prowess. Rabbi Jay Moses, Reverend Scotty McLennan, Cory Muscara, Reza Aslan, and Krista Tippett lent their unique religious perspectives. Anna Quindlen urged us to address the isolation of grief. Reb Rebele highlighted new developments in resilience research. Arianna Huffington reminded us that people read not just to learn but to hope. Craig and Kirsten Nevill-Manning showed up as they always do and weighed in on key questions of tone. Scott Tierney emphasized the power of investing in community before adversity strikes. Nola Barackman and Tessa Lyons-Laing called out the elephants in the book. Lauren Bohn interviewed Wafaa with a wonderful translator, Mohammed. Dan Levy and Grace Song taught us about resilient small businesses. Kara Swisher and Mellody Hobson helped us get key phrases right. Ricki Seidman stepped in to improve cohesion and clarity. Michael Lynton encouraged us to reflect on how this book connected to our previous writings. Colin Summers patiently answered daily questions about style and substance. And we give our most heartfelt thanks to Allison Grant, who not only shared her knowledge of mental health but also gave both of us her love and support throughout the entire writing process.

The team at Knopf jumped in from the get-go with enthusiasm that rose to ebullience (Paul Bogaards, we're looking at you). This book benefited tremendously from the diligent and passionate work of Peter Andersen, Lydia Buechler, Janet Cooke, Anna Dobben, Chris Gillespie, Erinn Hartman, Katherine Hourigan, Andy Hughes, James Kimball, Stephanie Kloss, Jennifer Kurdyla, Nicholas Latimer, Beth Meister, Lisa Montebello, Jennifer Olsen, Austin O'Malley, Cassandra Pappas, Lara Phan, Danielle Plafsky, Anne-Lise Spitzer, Anke Steinecke, Danielle Toth, and Amelia Zalcman. Ellen Feldman went above and beyond in shepherding our work from manuscript into print. We greatly appreciate the work of the extraordinary Amy Ryan, whose meticulousness was surpassed only by her patience for enduring endless emails about the Oxford comma.

Designing the book jacket was a labor of love for everyone involved. We thank Keith Hayes for his creativity and the talented team at Knopf who made the jacket possible: Kelly Blair, Carol Carson, Janet Hansen, Chip Kidd, Peter Mendelsund, and Oliver Munday. We also appreciate the invaluable contributions of John Ball, Holly Houk, Lauren Lamb, and Shawn Ritzenthaler at MiresBall.

We were fortunate to have the continuous support of the teams at WME and InkWell, especially Eric Zohn, Eliza Rothstein, Nathaniel Jacks, and Alexis Hurley. Huge thanks to Tracy Fisher for the expertise and dedication she brings to rolling this book out globally.

Many friends and colleagues read drafts and gave honest feedback. We are grateful for their time and their suggestions: Joy Bauer, Amanda Bennett, Jessica Bennett, David Bradley, Jon Cohen, Joanna Coles, Margaret Ewen, Anna Fieler, Stephanie Flanders, Adam Freed, Susan Gonzales, Don Graham, Nicole

Granet, Joel Kaplan, Rousseau Kazi, Mike Lewis, Sara Luchian, Schuyler Milender, Dan Rosensweig, Jim Santucci, Karen Kehela Sherwood, Anna Thompson, Clia Tierney, and Caroline Weber. A special shout-out to Larry Summers for making this the first book he ever read on his phone.

We relied heavily on research from outstanding social scientists, whose work informed our thinking and plays a central role in the book—especially on the three P's (Marty Seligman), social support (Peggy Thoits), self-compassion (Kristin Neff and Mark Leary), expressive writing (Jamie Pennebaker and Cindy Chung), job loss (Rick Price and Amiram Vinokur), post-traumatic growth and meaning (Richard Tedeschi, Lawrence Calhoun, and Amy Wrzesniewski), happiness and emotions (Jennifer Aaker, Mihaly Csikszentmihalyi, Dan Gilbert, Jonathan Haidt, Laura King, Brian Little, Richard Lucas, Sonja Lyubomirsky, C. R. Snyder, and Timothy Wilson), resilient kids (Marshall Duke, Carol Dweck, Gregory Elliott, Nicole Stephens, and David Yeager), collective resilience (Daniel Aldrich, Dan Gruber, Stevan Hobfoll, Michèle Lamont, and Michelle Meyer), failing and learning at work (Sue Ashford, Amy Edmondson, and Sabine Sonnentag), loss and grief (George Bonanno, Deborah Carr, Darrin Lehman, and Camille Wortman), and love and relationships (Arthur and Elaine Aron, Jane Dutton, and John and Julie Gottman).

Our deepest admiration goes to those who shared their stories in this book and on optionb.org. Most are members of clubs they didn't want to join, and we are so grateful that they offered their wisdom. We are inspired by their resilience and quest to find meaning and joy. On the days when the void closes in, we can all draw strength from their example.

Notes

INTRODUCTION

8   **"No one ever told me"**: C. S. Lewis, *A Grief Observed* (New York: Harper & Row, 1961).

9   **after losing a parent**: See, for example, Timothy J. Biblarz and Greg Gottainer, "Family Structure and Children's Success: A Comparison of Widowed and Divorced Single-Mother Families," *Journal of Marriage and Family* 62 (2000): 533–48; Kenneth S. Kendler, Michael C. Neale, Ronald C. Kessler, et al., "Childhood Parental Loss and Adult Psychopathology in Women: A Twin Study Perspective," *Archives of General Psychiatry* 49 (1992): 109–16; Jane D. McLeod, "Childhood Parental Loss and Adult Depression," *Journal of Health and Social Behavior* 32 (1991): 205–20.

9   **by six months, more than half of people**: George A. Bonanno, Camille B. Wortman, Darrin R. Lehman, et al., "Resilience to Loss and Chronic Grief: A Prospective Study from Preloss to 18-Months Postloss," *Journal of Personality and Social Psychology* 83 (2002): 1150–64. For further evidence, see George A. Bonanno, *The Other Side of Sadness: What the New Science of Bereavement Tells Us About Life After Loss* (New York: Basic Books, 2010).

12   **To fight for change tomorrow**: See Geoff DeVerteuil and Oleg Golubchikov, "Can Resilience Be Redeemed?," *City: Analysis of Urban Trends, Culture, Theory, Policy, Action* 20 (2016): 143–51; Markus Keck and Patrick Sakdapolrak, "What Is Social Resilience? Lessons Learned and Ways Forward," *Erdkunde* 67 (2013): 5–19.

I. BREATHING AGAIN

15   **"You must go on"**: Samuel Beckett, *The Unnamable* (New York: Grove Press, 1958).

16   **three P's can stunt recovery:** See Steven F. Maier and Martin E. P. Selig-
       man, "Learned Helplessness at Fifty: Insights from Neuroscience," *Psycho-
       logical Review* 123 (2016): 349–67; Martin E. P. Seligman, *Learned Optimism:
       How to Change Your Mind and Your Life* (New York: Pocket Books, 1991).

16   **makes people less likely to get depressed:** See Tracy R. G. Gladstone and
       Nadine J. Kaslow, "Depression and Attributions in Children and Adoles-
       cents: A Meta-Analytic Review," *Journal of Abnormal Child Psychology* 23
       (1995): 597–606.

16   **the three P's helped teachers:** Angela Lee Duckworth, Patrick D. Quinn,
       and Martin E. P. Seligman, "Positive Predictors of Teacher Effective-
       ness," *The Journal of Positive Psychology* 4 (2009): 540–47.

16   **It helped college varsity swimmers:** Martin E. P. Seligman, Susan Nolen-
       Hoeksema, Nort Thornton, and Karen Moe Thornton, "Explanatory
       Style as a Mechanism of Disappointing Athletic Performance," *Psycho-
       logical Science* 1 (1990): 143–46.

16   **it helped insurance salespeople:** Martin E. P. Seligman and Peter Schul-
       man, "Explanatory Style as a Predictor of Productivity and Quitting
       Among Life Insurance Sales Agents," *Journal of Personality and Social Psy-
       chology* 50 (1986): 832–38.

17   **it's common for rape victims to blame themselves:** Matt J. Gray, Jenni-
       fer E. Pumphrey, and Thomas W. Lombardo, "The Relationship Between
       Dispositional Pessimistic Attributional Style Versus Trauma-Specific
       Attributions and PTSD Symptoms," *Journal of Anxiety Disorders* 17 (2003):
       289–303; Ronnie Janoff-Bulman, "Characterological Versus Behavioral
       Self-Blame: Inquiries into Depression and Rape," *Journal of Personality and
       Social Psychology* 37 (1979): 1798–809.

18   **the thing I found myself saying most often:** Women tend to apologize
       more than men. See Karina Schumann and Michael Ross, "Why Women
       Apologize More than Men: Gender Differences in Thresholds for Per-
       ceiving Offensive Behavior," *Psychological Science* 21 (2010): 1649–55; Jar-
       rett T. Lewis, Gilbert R. Parra, and Robert Cohen, "Apologies in Close
       Relationships: A Review of Theory and Research," *Journal of Family The-
       ory and Review* 7 (2015): 47–61.

20   **only 60 percent of private sector workers:** Robert W. Van Giezen, "Paid
       Leave in Private Industry over the Past 20 Years," U.S. Bureau of Labor
       Statistics, *Beyond the Numbers* 2 (2013): www.bls.gov/opub/btn/volume-2
       /paid-leave-in-private-industry-over-the-past-20-years.htm. It is unaccept-
       able that in the United States parents have twelve weeks off when a child
       is born but only three days when a child dies, and that almost 30 percent of
       working mothers don't have access to paid leave: see http://scholars.unh
       .edu/cgi/viewcontent.cgi?article=1170&context=carsey. For a definition
       of paid leave, see Kristin Smith and Andrew Schaefer, "Who Cares for the
       Sick Kids? Parents' Access to Paid Time to Care for a Sick Child," Carsey
       Institute Issue Brief #51 (2012), accessed on December 16, 2016: http://
       scholars.unh.edu/cgi/viewcontent.cgi?article=1170&context=carsey.

20   **grief can interfere with their job performance:** Jane E. Dutton, Kris-
       tina M. Workman, and Ashley E. Hardin, "Compassion at Work," *Annual*

Review of Organizational Psychology and Organizational Behavior 1 (2014): 277–304.

20　**grief-related losses in productivity**: Darlene Gavron Stevens, "The Cost of Grief," *Chicago Tribune,* August 20, 2003: http://articles.chicagotribune .com/2003-08-20/business/0308200089_1_pet-loss-grief-emotions.

20　**long-term investment in employees pays off**: James H. Dulebohn, Janice C. Molloy, Shaun M. Pichler, and Brian Murray, "Employee Benefits: Literature Review and Emerging Issues," *Human Resource Management Review* 19 (2009): 86–103. See also Alex Edmans, "The Link Between Job Satisfaction and Firm Value, with Implications for Corporate Social Responsibility," *Academy of Management Perspectives* 26 (2012): 1–19; James K. Harter, Frank L. Schmidt, and Theodore L. Hayes, "Business-Unit-Level Relationship Between Employee Satisfaction, Employee Engagement, and Business Outcomes: A Meta-Analysis," *Journal of Applied Psychology* 87 (2002): 268–79.

21　**Studies of "affective forecasting"**: Daniel T. Gilbert, Elizabeth C. Pinel, Timothy D. Wilson, and Stephen J. Blumberg, "Immune Neglect: A Source of Durability Bias in Affective Forecasting," *Journal of Personality and Social Psychology* 75 (1998): 617–38.

21　**we tend to overestimate**: Timothy D. Wilson and Daniel T. Gilbert, "Affective Forecasting: Knowing What to Want," *Current Directions in Psychological Science* 14 (2005): 131–34; Daniel T. Gilbert, *Stumbling on Happiness* (New York: Knopf, 2006).

21　**Assistant professors thought being denied university tenure**: Gilbert et al., "Immune Neglect."

21　**College students believed they would be miserable**: Elizabeth W. Dunn, Timothy D. Wilson, and Daniel T. Gilbert, "Location, Location, Location: The Misprediction of Satisfaction in Housing Lotteries," *Personality and Social Psychology Bulletin* 29 (2003): 1421–32.

22　**cognitive behavioral therapy technique**: See the Beck Institute for Cognitive Behavior Therapy: www.beckinstitute.org.

23　**"Part of every misery"**: C. S. Lewis, *A Grief Observed* (New York: Harper & Row, 1961).

24　**"making friends with our own demons"**: Pema Chödrön, *When Things Fall Apart: Heart Advice for Difficult Times* (Boston: Shambhala, 1997).

25　**good idea to think about how much worse**: Alex M. Wood, Jeffrey J. Froh, and Adam W. A. Geraghty, "Gratitude and Well-Being: A Review and Theoretical Integration," *Clinical Psychology Review* 30 (2010): 890–905; Laura J. Kray, Katie A. Liljenquist, Adam D. Galinsky, et al., "From What *Might* Have Been to What *Must* Have Been: Counterfactual Thinking Creates Meaning," *Journal of Personality and Social Psychology* 98 (2010): 106–18; Karl Halvor Teigen, "Luck, Envy, and Gratitude: It Could Have Been Different," *Scandinavian Journal of Psychology* 38 (1997): 313–23; Minkyung Koo, Sara B. Algoe, Timothy D. Wilson, and Daniel T. Gilbert, "It's a Wonderful Life: Mentally Subtracting Positive Events Improves People's Affective States, Contrary to Their Affective Forecasts," *Journal of Personality and Social Psychology* 95 (2008): 1217–24.

26 **Psychologists asked a group of people to make a weekly list**: Robert A. Emmons and Michael E. McCullough, "Counting Blessings Versus Burdens: An Experimental Investigation of Gratitude and Subjective Well-Being in Daily Life," *Journal of Personality and Social Psychology* 84 (2003): 377–89.

26 **People who enter the workforce**: Emily C. Bianchi, "The Bright Side of Bad Times: The Affective Advantages of Entering the Workforce in a Recession," *Administrative Science Quarterly* 58 (2013): 587–623.

26 **Sixty percent of Americans have faced an event**: "Americans' Financial Security: Perception and Reality," The Pew Charitable Trusts, accessed on December 14, 2016: www.pewtrusts.org/en/research-and-analysis /issue-briefs/2015/02/americans-financial-security-perceptions-and -reality.

26 **The death of a partner often brings**: Mariko Lin Chang, *Shortchanged: Why Women Have Less Wealth and What Can Be Done About It* (New York: Oxford University Press, 2010).

26 **often left without money for basic needs**: Alicia H. Munnell and Nadia S. Karamcheva, "Why Are Widows So Poor?," Center for Retirement Research at Boston College Brief IB#7-9, accessed on December 14, 2016: http://crr.bc.edu/briefs/why-are-widows-so-poor/.

26 **Of the 258 million**: "World Widow's Report," The Loomba Foundation, accessed on March 11, 2017: http://theloombafoundation.org/home/.

2. KICKING THE ELEPHANT OUT OF THE ROOM

31 **non-question-asking friend**: Tim Urban, "10 Types of Odd Friendships You're Probably Part Of," *Wait but Why,* December 2014: http://wait-butwhy.com/2014/12/10-types-odd-friendships-youre-probably-part. html. For evidence that people are better liked when they ask more questions, see Karen Huang, Mike Yeomans, Alison Wood Brooks, et al., "It Doesn't Hurt to Ask: Question-Asking Encourages Self-Disclosure and Increases Liking," *Journal of Personality and Social Psychology* (in press).

33 **"Our child dies a second time"**: Mitch Carmody, quoted in Linton Weeks, "Now We Are Alone: Living On Without Our Sons," *All Things Considered,* NPR, September 3, 2010: www.npr.org/templates/story/story .php?storyId=128977776.

33 **the term "mum effect"**: Sidney Rosen and Abraham Tesser, "On Reluctance to Communicate Undesirable Information: The MUM Effect," *Sociometry* 33 (1970): 253–63.

34 **Doctors hold back**: Joshua D. Margolis and Andrew Molinsky, "Navigating the Bind of Necessary Evils: Psychological Engagement and the Production of Interpersonally Sensitive Behavior," *Academy of Management Journal* 51 (2008): 847–72; Jayson L. Dibble, "Breaking Bad News in the Provider-Recipient Context: Understanding the Hesitation to Share Bad News from the Sender's Perspective," in *Medical Communication in Clinical Contexts,* ed. Benjamin Bates and Rukhsana Ahmed (Dubuque, IA: Kendall Hunt Publishing, 2012). See also Walter F. Baile, Robert Buckman, Renato Lenzi,

et al., "SPIKES—A Six-Step Protocol for Delivering Bad News: Application to the Patient with Cancer," *The Oncologist* 5 (2000): 302–11.

34 **give themselves painful electric shocks**: Timothy D. Wilson, David A. Reinhard, Erin C. Westgate, et al., "Just Think: The Challenges of the Disengaged Mind," *Science* 345 (2014): 75–77.

34 **psychologists literally call them "openers"**: Lynn C. Miller, John H. Berg, and Richard L. Archer, "Openers: Individuals Who Elicit Intimate Self-Disclosure," *Journal of Personality and Social Psychology* 44 (1983): 1234–44.

35 **People who have faced adversity tend to express**: Daniel Lim and David DeSteno, "Suffering and Compassion: The Links Among Adverse Life Experiences, Empathy, Compassion, and Prosocial Behavior," *Emotion* 16 (2016): 175–82. Note that when people have conquered a distressing event and see others failing to do so, they may be less compassionate: Rachel L. Ruttan, Mary-Hunter McDonnell, and Loran F. Nordgren, "Having 'Been There' Doesn't Mean I Care: When Prior Experience Reduces Compassion for Emotional Distress," *Journal of Personality and Social Psychology* 108 (2015): 610–22.

35 **"those of us who recognize in one another"**: Anna Quindlen, "Public and Private: Life After Death," *The New York Times*, May 4, 1994: www.nytimes.com/1994/05/04/opinion/public-private-life-after-death.html.

35 **Military veterans, rape victims, and parents**: Darrin R. Lehman, John H. Ellard, and Camille B. Wortman, "Social Support for the Bereaved: Recipients' and Providers' Perspectives on What Is Helpful," *Journal of Consulting and Clinical Psychology* 54 (1986): 438–46.

36 **In China and Japan, the ideal emotional state**: Jeanne L. Tsai, "Ideal Affect: Cultural Causes and Behavioral Consequences," *Perspectives on Psychological Science* 2 (2007): 242–59.

36 **"American culture demands that the answer"**: David Caruso, quoted in Julie Beck, "How to Get Better at Expressing Emotions," *The Atlantic*, November 18, 2015: www.theatlantic.com/health/archive/2015/11/how-to-get-better-at-expressing-emotions/416493/.

36 **"a whisper in the world"**: Quindlen, "Public and Private."

38 **I poured my emotions into a post**: Sheryl Sandberg, Facebook post, June 3, 2015: www.facebook.com/sheryl/posts/10155617891025177:0.

39 **opening up about traumatic events**: For a review, see James W. Pennebaker and Joshua M. Smyth, *Opening Up by Writing It Down: How Expressive Writing Improves Health and Eases Emotional Pain* (New York: Guilford, 2016). For more details, see chapter 4.

41 **the challenges of coming out in immigrant families**: Anthony C. Ocampo, "The Gay Second Generation: Sexual Identity and the Family Relations of Filipino and Latino Gay Men," *Journal of Ethnic and Migration Studies* 40 (2014): 155–73; Anthony C. Ocampo, "Making Masculinity: Negotiations of Gender Presentation Among Latino Gay Men," *Latino Studies* 10 (2012): 448–72.

42 **"It was the loneliness and isolation I felt"**: Emily McDowell, quoted in Kristin Hohendal, "A Cancer Survivor Designs the Cards She Wishes She'd Received from Friends and Family," *The Eye*, May 6, 2015: www.slate.com/blogs/the_eye/2015/05/06/empathy_cards_by_emily_mcdowell_are_greeting_cards_designed_for_cancer_patients.html.

42 Emily created "empathy cards": http://emilymcdowell.com/. See also Kelsey Crowe and Emily McDowell, *There Is No Good Card for This: What to Say and Do When Life Is Scary, Awful, and Unfair to People You Love* (New York: HarperOne, 2017).

43 "When you're faced with tragedy": Tim Lawrence, "8 Simple Words to Say When Someone You Love Is Grieving," *Upworthy*, December 17, 2015: www.upworthy.com/8-simple-words-to-say-when-when-someone-you -love-is-grieving.

3. THE PLATINUM RULE OF FRIENDSHIP

46 In classic experiments on stress: David C. Glass and Jerome Singer, "Behavioral Consequences of Adaptation to Controllable and Uncontrollable Noise," *Journal of Experimental Social Psychology* 7 (1971): 244–57; David C. Glass and Jerome E. Singer, "Experimental Studies of Uncontrollable and Unpredictable Noise," *Representative Research in Social Psychology* 4 (1973): 165–83.

47 When people are in pain, they need a button: Brian R. Little, *Me, Myself, and Us: The Science of Personality and the Art of Well-Being* (New York: Public Affairs, 2014).

47 There are two different emotional responses: C. Daniel Batson, Jim Fultz, and Patricia A. Schoenrade, "Distress and Empathy: Two Qualitatively Distinct Vicarious Emotions with Different Motivational Consequences," *Journal of Personality* 55 (1987): 19–39.

47 "As some friends checked in daily": Allen Rucker, *The Best Seat in the House: How I Woke Up One Tuesday and Was Paralyzed for Life* (New York: HarperCollins, 2007).

50 In one experiment, people were asked: Loran F. Nordgren, Mary-Hunter McDonnell, and George Loewenstein, "What Constitutes Torture? Psychological Impediments to an Objective Evaluation of Enhanced Interrogation Tactics," *Psychological Science* 22 (2011): 689–94.

51 the Platinum Rule: This is a term that has been attributed to many sources. One of the best descriptions comes from Karl Popper's writing. "The golden rule is a good standard which can perhaps even be improved by doing unto others, wherever possible, as *they* would be done by": Karl Popper, *The Open Society and Its Enemies*, vol. 2 (New York: Routledge, 1945/1966).

51 "while well meaning, this gesture": Bruce Feiler, "How to Be a Friend in Deed," *The New York Times*, February 6, 2015: www.nytimes.com/2015 /02/08/style/how-to-be-a-friend-in-deed.html.

52 "Some things in life cannot be fixed": Megan Devine, Refuge in Grief: Emotionally Intelligent Grief Support, accessed on December 14, 2016: www.refugeingrief.com/.

52 Psychologists put teenage girls under stress: Jessica P. Lougheed, Peter Koval, and Tom Hollenstein, "Sharing the Burden: The Interpersonal Regulation of Emotional Arousal in Mother-Daughter Dyads," *Emotion* 16 (2016): 83–93.

52 the "ring theory": Susan Silk and Barry Goldman, "How Not to Say the Wrong Thing," *Los Angeles Times*, April 7, 2013: http://articles.latimes .com/2013/apr/07/opinion/la-oe-0407-silk-ring-theory-20130407.

55　the five stages of grief: Elisabeth Kübler-Ross, *On Death and Dying* (New York: Routledge, 1969).

55　these are not five stages: Holly G. Prigerson and Paul K. Maciejewski, "Grief and Acceptance as Opposite Sides of the Same Coin: Setting a Research Agenda to Study Peaceful Acceptance of Loss," *The British Journal of Psychiatry* 193 (2008): 435–37. See also Margaret Stroebe and Henk Schut, "The Dual Process Model of Coping with Bereavement: Rationale and Description," *Death Studies* 23 (1999): 197–224. As social worker Carole Geithner explained to us, stage models "also minimize the individuality and diversity of how people grieve. There are different grieving styles and coping strategies. Grief models create problems when they become prescriptive. More current models emphasize individuality. There is an understandable wish for models because we want reassurance, to know there is an endpoint, a game plan, some predictability, but there is a downside: They are not true to the reality of grief. They provide illusory comfort. Each person's loss is different."

56　As people mature, they focus: Laura L. Carstensen, Derek M. Isaacowitz, and Susan T. Charles, "Taking Time Seriously: A Theory of Socioemotional Selectivity," *American Psychologist* 54 (1999): 165–81.

56　the quality of friendships becomes: Cheryl L. Carmichael, Harry T. Reis, and Paul R. Duberstein, "In Your 20s It's Quantity, in Your 30s It's Quality: The Prognostic Value of Social Activity Across 30 Years of Adulthood," *Psychology and Aging* 30 (2015): 95–105.

56　"Footprints in the Sand": Allegorical poem published in various versions. See, for example, http://www.footprints-inthe-sand.com/index .php?page=Main.php.

4. SELF-COMPASSION AND SELF-CONFIDENCE

58　nearly one in four Americans has a criminal history: Matthew Friedman, "Just Facts: As Many Americans Have Criminal Records as College Diplomas," Brennan Center for Justice, November 17, 2015: www .brennancenter.org/blog/just-facts-many-americans-have-criminal -records-college-diplomas; Thomas P. Bonczar and Allen J. Beck, "Lifetime Likelihood of Going to State or Federal Prison," Bureau of Justice Statistics, special report NCJ 160092, March 6, 1997: www.nij.gov/topics /corrections/reentry/Pages/employment.aspx.

58　criminal records make it difficult to get jobs: Only 40 percent of employers would "definitely" or "probably" hire applicants with criminal records. And in an experiment using otherwise identical résumés, job applicants with a criminal record were half as likely to get a callback. See John Schmitt and Kris Warner, "Ex-Offenders and the Labor Market," *The Journal of Labor and Society* 14 (2011): 87–109; Steven Raphael, *The New Scarlet Letter? Negotiating the U.S. Labor Market with a Criminal Record* (Kalamazoo, MI: Upjohn Institute Press, 2014).

59　The governor of Texas honored Catherine's work: www.legis.state.tx .us/tlodocs/81R/billtext/html/HR00175I.htm and www.kbtx.com/home /headlines/7695432.html?site=full. Along with our interviews with

Catherine Hoke, details and quotes are drawn from Kris Frieswick, "Ex-Cons Relaunching Lives as Entrepreneurs," *Inc.*, May 29, 2012: www.inc.com/magazine/201206/kris-frieswick/catherine-rohr-defy-ventures-story-of-redemption.html; Leonardo Blair, "Christian Venture Capitalist Defies Sex Scandal with God's Calling," *The Christian Post*, October 31, 2015: www.christianpost.com/news/christian-venture-capitalist-defies-sex-scandal-with-gods-calling-148873/; Ryan Young, "CCU's Moglia Teaching 'Life After Football,'" *Myrtle Beach Online*, August 22, 2015: www.myrtlebeachonline.com/sports/college/sun-belt/coastal-carolina-university/article31924596.html; Jessica Weisberg, "Shooting Straight," *The New Yorker*, February 10, 2014: www.newyorker.com/magazine/2014/02/10/shooting-straight.

60   **Self-compassion comes from recognizing**: Kristin D. Neff, "The Development and Validation of a Scale to Measure Self-Compassion," *Self and Identity* 2 (2003): 223–50. See also Kristin Neff, *Self-Compassion: The Proven Power of Being Kind to Yourself* (New York: William Morrow, 2011).

60   **In a study of people whose marriages fell apart**: David A. Sbarra, Hillary L. Smith, and Matthias R. Mehl, "When Leaving Your Ex, Love Yourself: Observational Ratings of Self-Compassion Predict the Course of Emotional Recovery Following Marital Separation," *Psychological Science* 23 (2012): 261–69.

60   **For soldiers returning from war**: Regina Hiraoka, Eric C. Meyer, Nathan A. Kimbrel, et al., "Self-Compassion as a Prospective Predictor of PTSD Symptom Severity Among Trauma-Exposed U.S. Iraq and Afghanistan War Veterans," *Journal of Traumatic Stress* 28 (2015): 127–33.

60   **Self-compassion is associated with greater happiness**: Kristin D. Neff, "Self-Compassion, Self-Esteem, and Well-Being," *Social and Personality Psychology Compass* 5 (2011): 1–12; Angus Macbeth and Andrew Gumley, "Exploring Compassion: A Meta-Analysis of the Association Between Self-Compassion and Psychopathology," *Clinical Psychology Review* 32 (2012): 545–52; Nicholas T. Van Dam, Sean C. Sheppard, John P. Forsyth, and Mitch Earleywine, "Self-Compassion Is a Better Predictor than Mindfulness of Symptom Severity and Quality of Life in Mixed Anxiety and Depression," *Journal of Anxiety Disorders* 25 (2011): 123–30; Michelle E. Neely, Diane L. Schallert, Sarojanni S. Mohammed, et al., "Self-Kindness When Facing Stress: The Role of Self-Compassion, Goal Regulation, and Support in College Students' Well-Being," *Motivation and Emotion* 33 (2009): 88–97.

60   **Both women and men can benefit**: Lisa M. Yarnell, Rose E. Stafford, Kristin D. Neff, et al., "Meta-Analysis of Gender Differences in Self-Compassion," *Self and Identity* 14 (2015): 499–520; Levi R. Baker and James K. McNulty, "Self-Compassion and Relationship Maintenance: The Moderating Roles of Conscientiousness and Gender," *Journal of Personality and Social Psychology* 100 (2011): 853–73. Importantly, self-compassion does not help relationships—and may hurt them—if people are not motivated to improve upon their mistakes.

60   **"can be an antidote to the cruelty"**: Mark Leary, "Don't Beat Yourself Up," *Aeon*, June 20, 2016: https://aeon.co/essays/learning-to-be-kind-to-yourself-has-remarkable-benefits. See also Meredith L. Terry and Mark

Leary, "Self-Compassion, Self-Regulation, and Health," *Self and Identity* 10 (2011): 352–62.

61 **Instead of thinking "if only I weren't"**: Paula M. Niedenthal, June Price Tangney, and Igor Gavanski, "'If Only I Weren't' Versus 'If Only I Hadn't': Distinguishing Shame and Guilt in Counterfactual Thinking," *Journal of Personality and Social Psychology* 67 (1994): 585–95.

61 **Blaming our actions rather than our character**: Ronnie Janoff-Bulman, "Characterological Versus Behavioral Self-Blame: Inquiries into Depression and Rape," *Journal of Personality and Social Psychology* 37 (1979): 1798–809.

61 **"the gift that keeps giving"**: Erma Bombeck, *Motherhood: The Second Oldest Profession* (New York: McGraw-Hill, 1983).

61 **guilt keeps us striving**: June Price Tangney and Ronda L. Dearing, *Shame and Guilt* (New York: Guilford, 2002).

61 **Among college students, the shame-prone**: Ronda L. Dearing, Jeffrey Stuewig, and June Price Tangney, "On the Importance of Distinguishing Shame from Guilt: Relations to Problematic Alcohol and Drug Use," *Addictive Behaviors* 30 (2005): 1392–404.

61 **Prisoners who felt ashamed**: Daniela Hosser, Michael Windzio, and Werner Greve, "Guilt and Shame as Predictors of Recidivism: A Longitudinal Study with Young Prisoners," *Criminal Justice and Behavior* 35 (2008): 138–52. See also June P. Tangney, Jeffrey Stuewig, and Andres G. Martinez, "Two Faces of Shame: The Roles of Shame and Guilt in Predicting Recidivism," *Psychological Science* 25 (2014): 799–805.

61 **Elementary and middle school kids**: June Price Tangney, Patricia E. Wagner, Deborah Hill-Barlow, et al., "Relation of Shame and Guilt to Constructive Versus Destructive Responses to Anger Across the Lifespan," *Journal of Personality and Social Psychology* 70 (1996): 797–809.

61 **"we are all broken by something"**: Bryan Stevenson, *Just Mercy: A Story of Justice and Redemption* (New York: Spiegel & Grau, 2014).

62 **Writing can be a powerful tool**: Mark R. Leary, Eleanor B. Tate, Claire E. Adams, et al., "Self-Compassion and Reactions to Unpleasant Self-Relevant Events: The Implications of Treating Oneself Kindly," *Journal of Personality and Social Psychology* 92 (2007): 887–904.

62 **Turning feelings into words can help**: For reviews, see James W. Pennebaker and Joshua M. Smyth, *Opening Up by Writing It Down: How Expressive Writing Improves Health and Eases Emotional Pain* (New York: Guilford, 2016); Joanne Frattaroli, "Experimental Disclosure and Its Moderators: A Meta-Analysis," *Psychological Bulletin* 132 (2006): 823–65; Joshua M. Smyth, "Written Emotional Expression: Effect Sizes, Outcome Types, and Moderating Variables," *Journal of Consulting and Clinical Psychology* 66 (1998): 174–84. For evidence that it gets worse before it gets better, see Antonio Pascual-Leone, Nikita Yeryomenko, Orrin-Porter Morrison, et al., "Does Feeling Bad Lead to Feeling Good? Arousal Patterns During Expressive Writing," *Review of General Psychology* 20 (2016): 336–47. This body of research also suggests that journaling works best when we write privately, just for ourselves, and describe facts and feelings; that men tend to benefit a bit more from journaling than women since they're more likely to bottle up their feelings; and that people with more health problems

and a history of trauma or stress show the greatest benefits. And most importantly, there is a big difference between organizing your thoughts and feelings about an upsetting experience and ruminating about them— trying to make sense of them seems to help, whereas dwelling on them does not. "Many people often find that they are thinking about, dreaming about, or talking about an upsetting event in the past too much. They also find that others don't want to hear about it," psychologist Darrin Lehman told us. "It is these people that might try expressive writing. It's not a panacea, it's free, and the effect sizes are modest. If it doesn't seem to help, these people should stop writing and seek some other treatment."

63 **Labeling negative emotions**: Matthew D. Lieberman, Naomi I. Eisen- berger, Molly J. Crockett, et al., "Putting Feelings into Words," *Psy- chological Science* 18 (2007): 421–28; Lisa Feldman Barrett, "Are You in Despair? That's Good," *The New York Times*, June 3, 2016: www.nytimes .com/2016/06/05/opinion/sunday/are-you-in-despair-thats-good.html.

63 **those who labeled their fear**: Katharina Kircanski, Matthew D. Lieber- man, and Michelle G. Craske, "Feelings into Words: Contributions of Language to Exposure Therapy," *Psychological Science* 23 (2012): 1086–91.

63 **journaling can backfire**: Along with Pennebaker and Smyth's *Opening Up by Writing It Down*, see the literature on critical incident stress debrief- ing: Timothy D. Wilson, *Redirect: The Surprising New Science of Psychologi- cal Change* (New York: Little, Brown, 2011); Jonathan I. Bisson, Peter L. Jenkins, Julie Alexander, and Carol Bannister, "Randomised Controlled Trial of Psychological Debriefing for Victims of Acute Burn Trauma," *The British Journal of Psychiatry* 171 (1997): 78–81; Benedict Carey, "Sept. 11 Revealed Psychology's Limits, Review Finds," *The New York Times*, July 28, 2011: www.nytimes.com/2011/07/29/health/research/29psych.html.

63 **After loss, it appears that writing**: Karolijne van der Houwen, Henk Schut, Jan van den Bout, et al., "The Efficacy of a Brief Internet-Based Self-Help Intervention for the Bereaved," *Behaviour Research and Therapy* 48 (2010): 359–67.

63 **talking into a voice recorder works**: James W. Pennebaker and Janel D. Seagal, "Forming a Story: The Health Benefits of Narrative," *Journal of Clinical Psychology* 55 (1999): 1243–54.

64 **Self-confidence is critical**: Alexander D. Stajkovic, "Development of a Core Confidence–Higher Order Construct," *Journal of Applied Psychology* 91 (2006): 1208–24; Timothy A. Judge and Joyce E. Bono, "Relationship of Core Self-Evaluation Traits—Self-Esteem, Generalized Self-Efficacy, Locus of Control, and Emotional Stability—with Job Satisfaction and Job Performance: A Meta-Analysis," *Journal of Applied Psychology* 86 (2001): 80–92.

65 **the impostor syndrome**: Mark R. Leary, Katharine M. Patton, Amy E. Orlando, and Wendy Wagoner Funk, "The Impostor Phenomenon: Self- Perceptions, Reflected Appraisals, and Interpersonal Strategies," *Journal of Personality* 68 (2000): 725–56.

65 **I gave a TED talk**: Sheryl Sandberg, "Why We Have Too Few Women Leaders," TED Women, December 2010: www.ted.com/talks/sheryl _sandberg_why_we_have_too_few_women_leaders.

65 trauma can also lead to self-doubt: Edna B. Foa and Elizabeth A. Meadows, "Psychosocial Treatments for Posttraumatic Stress Disorder: A Critical Review," *Annual Review of Psychology* 48 (1997): 449–80. See also Patricia A. Resick and Monica K. Schnike, "Cognitive Processing Therapy for Sexual Assault Victims," *Journal of Consulting and Clinical Psychology* 60 (1992): 748–56.

67 life can only be understood backward: Søren Kierkegaard, *Papers and Journals: A Selection* (New York: Penguin, 1996); Daniel W. Conway and K. E. Gover, *Søren Kierkegaard*, vol. 1 (New York: Taylor & Francis, 2002).

68 "small wins": Karl E. Weick, "Small Wins: Redefining the Scale of Social Problems," *American Psychologist* 39 (1984): 40–49; Teresa Amabile and Steven Kramer, *The Progress Principle: Using Small Wins to Ignite Joy, Engagement, and Creativity at Work* (Boston: Harvard Business Review Press, 2011).

68 people wrote down three things that went well: Martin E. P. Seligman, Tracy A. Steen, Nansook Park, and Christopher Peterson, "Positive Psychology Progress: Empirical Validation of Interventions," *American Psychologist* 60 (2005): 410–21.

68 In a more recent study: Joyce E. Bono, Theresa M. Glomb, Winny Shen, et al., "Building Positive Resources: Effects of Positive Events and Positive Reflection on Work Stress and Health," *Academy of Management Journal* 56 (2013): 1601–27.

68 counting our blessings doesn't boost our confidence: Adam M. Grant and Jane E. Dutton, "Beneficiary or Benefactor: Are People More Prosocial When They Reflect on Receiving or Giving?," *Psychological Science* 23 (2012): 1033–39. When university fund-raisers kept a journal for a few days detailing how they'd been helpful to colleagues, their hourly effort increased by 29 percent over the next two weeks.

70 cancer survivors were less likely to get called back: Larry R. Martinez, Craig D. White, Jenessa R. Shapiro, and Michelle R. Hebl, "Selection BIAS: Stereotypes and Discrimination Related to Having a History of Cancer," *Journal of Applied Psychology* 101 (2016): 122–28.

70 nearly 45 million people: "India Employed Persons," Trading Economics, accessed on March 11, 2017: http://www.tradingeconomics.com/india/employed-persons.

70 nearly 24 million: "February 2015: Euro Area Unemployment Rate at 11.3," Eurostat, accessed on March 11, 2017: http://ec.europa.eu/eurostat/documents/2995521/6764147/3-31032015-AP-EN.pdf/6e77d229-9c87-4671-9a52-b6450099597a.

70 In South Africa: "Labor Market Dynamics in South Africa, 2015," Statistics South Africa, accessed on March 11, 2017: www.statssa.gov.za/?p=8615.

70 Not only does loss of income: Richard H. Price, Jin Nam Choi, and Amiram D. Vinokur, "Links in the Chain of Adversity Following Job Loss: How Financial Strain and Loss of Personal Control Lead to Depression, Impaired Functioning, and Poor Health," *Journal of Occupational Health Psychology* 7 (2002): 302–12.

71 By robbing people of a sense of control: Eileen Y. Chou, Bidhan L. Parmar, and Adam D. Galinsky, "Economic Insecurity Increases Physical Pain," *Psychological Science* 27 (2016): 443–54.

71 **stress can spill over into personal relationships**: Amiram D. Vinokur, Richard H. Price, and Robert D. Caplan, "Hard Times and Hurtful Partners: How Financial Strain Affects Depression and Relationship Satisfaction of Unemployed Persons and Their Spouses," *Journal of Personality and Social Psychology* 71 (1996): 166–79.

71 **To help people suffering**: Amiram D. Vinokur, Michelle van Ryn, Edward M. Gramlich, and Richard H. Price, "Long-Term Follow-Up and Benefit-Cost Analysis of the Jobs Program: A Preventive Intervention for the Unemployed," *Journal of Applied Psychology* 76 (1991): 213–19; "The Jobs Project for the Unemployed: Update," Michigan Prevention Research Center, accessed on December 15, 2016: www.isr.umich.edu/src/seh /mprc/jobsupdt.html.

71 **programs like this can make a difference**: Songqi Liu, Jason L. Huang, and Mo Wang, "Effectiveness of Job Search Interventions: A Meta-Analytic Review," *Psychological Bulletin* 140 (2014): 1009–41.

72 **the number of single mothers**: Sarah Jane Glynn, "Breadwinning Mothers, Then and Now," Center for American Progress, June 20, 2014: www .americanprogress.org/issues/labor/report/2014/06/20/92355/bread winning-mothers-then-and-now/.

72 **Worldwide, 15 percent**: OECD, "Families are Changing" in *Doing Better for Families,* accessed on March 11, 2017: www.keepeek.com/ Digital-Asset-Management/oecd/social-issues-migration-health/doing-better-for-families/families-are-changing_9789264098732-3-en#page1.

72 **The costs of placing**: Child Care Aware of America, "Parents and the High Cost of Child Care: 2015 Report": http://usa.childcareaware.org /wp-content/uploads/2016/05/Parents-and-the-High-Cost-of-Child -Care-2015-FINAL.pdf.

72 **single mothers have higher rates**: Institute for Women's Policy Research, "Status of Women in the States," April 8, 2015: http://statusofwomendata. org/press-releases/in-every-u-s-state-women-including-millennials-are-more-likely-than-men-to-live-in-poverty-despite-gains-in-higher-education/; Social Policy Research Centre, "Poverty in Australia 2016," accessed on March 11, 2017: www.acoss.org.au/wp-content/ uploads/2016/10/Poverty-in-Australia-2016.pdf; Yekaterina Chzhen and Jonathan Bradshaw, "Lone Parents Poverty and Policy in the European Union," *Journal of European Social Policy* 22 (2012) 487–506; United Nations Department of Economic and Social Affairs, "The World's Women 2015: Trends and Statistics," accessed on March 11, 2017: https://unstats. un.org/unsd/gender/downloads/WorldsWomen2015_report.pdf.

72 **almost twice as likely to be poor**: United States Census Bureau, "Historical Poverty Tables: People and Families—1959 to 2015," accessed on December 19, 2016: www.census.gov/data/tables/time-series/demo /income-poverty/historical-poverty-people.html.

72 **Almost a third of single mothers**: United States Department of Agriculture, "Key Statistics & Graphics," accessed on December 16, 2016: www .ers.usda.gov/topics/food-nutrition-assistance/food-security-in-the-us /key-statistics-graphics.aspx.

72   **Stand Up for Kids campaign**: After family food distributions the school
     experienced a year-over-year reduction in student absenteeism of 32 per-
     cent, and monthly health complaints dropped by 72 percent. Presentation
     by Sonya Arriola, president of Sacred Heart Nativity Schools, accessed on
     December 19, 2016.

72   **Stand Up for Kids campaign**: After family food distributions the school
     experienced a year-over-year reduction in student absenteeism of 32 per-
     cent, and monthly health complaints dropped by 72 percent. Presentation
     by Sonya Arriola, president of Sacred Heart Nativity Schools, accessed on
     December 19, 2016.

73   **In Australia, maternity leave**: International Labour Organization, "Mater-
     nity and Paternity at Work: Law and Practice across the World," (Geneva:
     International Labour Organization, 2014), accessed on March 11, 2017:
     www.ilo.org/wcmsp5/groups/public/---dgreports/---dcomm/---publ/
     documents/publication/wcms_242615.pdf; Lakshmi Lingam and Aruna
     Kanchi, "Women's Work, Maternity and Public Policy" (Hyderabad; Tata
     Institute of Social Sciences, 2014).

     Australia offers 18 weeks of maternity leave, paid only at the federal mini-
     mum wage. India offers new mothers 13 weeks of partially paid maternity
     leave. However, since the majority of workers are in informal sectors, they are
     beyond the reach of formal benefits programs. As a result, it is estimated that
     less than one percent of women workers are eligible for maternity benefits.
     South Africa provides four months of maternity leave, paid at a maximum of
     60 percent of a woman's pre-maternity leave earnings. In both the U.S. and
     South Africa, there are minimum working hours in order for a woman to be
     eligible for maternity leave. The United Kingdom offers 52 weeks of mater-
     nity leave, composed of a combination of paid and unpaid time. The first six
     weeks are paid by employers and mostly reimbursed by public funds. Weeks
     7–39 are paid at a discounted rate and weeks 40–52 are unpaid.

73   **offering support through personal hardships**: Adam M. Grant, Jane E.
     Dutton, and Brent D. Rosso, "Giving Commitment: Employee Support
     Programs and the Prosocial Sensemaking Process," *Academy of Manage-
     ment Journal* 51 (2008): 898–918.

5. BOUNCING FORWARD

77   **"In the depths of winter"**: Albert Camus, *Lyrical and Critical Essays* (New
     York: Vintage, 1970).

77   **"In a few short moments"**: Joseph E. Kasper, "Co-Destiny: A Conceptual
     Goal for Parental Bereavement and the Call for a 'Positive Turn' in the
     Scientific Study of the Parental Bereavement Process," unpublished mas-
     ter's thesis, University of Pennsylvania, 2013.

77   **"When we are no longer able to change"**: Viktor Frankl, *Man's Search for
     Meaning* (New York: Pocket Books, 1959).

78   **experienced post-traumatic** *growth:* Richard G. Tedeschi and Law-
     rence G. Calhoun, *Helping Bereaved Parents: A Clinician's Guide* (New York:
     Routledge, 2003).

78   **Psychologists went on to study**: For reviews, see Richard G. Tedeschi and Lawrence G. Calhoun, "Posttraumatic Growth: Conceptual Foundations and Empirical Evidence," *Psychological Inquiry* 15 (2004): 1–18; Vicki S. Helgeson, Kerry A. Reynolds, and Patricia L. Tomich, "A Meta-Analytic Review of Benefit Finding and Growth," *Journal of Consulting and Clinical Psychology* 74 (2006): 797–816; Gabriele Prati and Luca Pietrantoni, "Optimism, Social Support, and Coping Strategies as Factors Contributing to Posttraumatic Growth: A Meta-Analysis," *Journal of Loss and Trauma* 14 (2009): 364–88.

78   **victims of sexual assault and abuse**: Patricia Frazier, Ty Tashiro, Margit Berman, et al., "Correlates of Levels and Patterns of Positive Life Changes Following Sexual Assault," *Journal of Consulting and Clinical Psychology* 72 (2004): 19–30; Amanda R. Cobb, Richard G. Tedeschi, Lawrence G. Calhoun, and Arnie Cann, "Correlates of Posttraumatic Growth in Survivors of Intimate Partner Violence," *Journal of Traumatic Stress* 19 (2006): 895–903.

78   **refugees and prisoners of war**: Steve Powell, Rita Rosner, Will Butollo, et al., "Posttraumatic Growth After War: A Study with Former Refugees and Displaced People in Sarajevo," *Journal of Clinical Psychology* 59 (2003): 71–83; Zahava Solomon and Rachel Dekel, "Posttraumatic Stress Disorder and Posttraumatic Growth Among Israeli Ex-POWs," *Journal of Traumatic Stress* 20 (2007): 303–12.

78   **survivors of accidents, natural disasters**: Tanja Zoellner, Sirko Rabe, Anke Karl, and Andreas Maercker, "Posttraumatic Growth in Accident Survivors: Openness and Optimism as Predictors of Its Constructive or Illusory Sides," *Journal of Clinical Psychology* 64 (2008): 245–63; Cheryl H. Cryder, Ryan P. Kilmer, Richard G. Tedeschi, and Lawrence G. Calhoun, "An Exploratory Study of Posttraumatic Growth in Children Following a Natural Disaster," *American Journal of Orthopsychiatry* 76 (2006): 65–69.

78   **severe injuries, and illnesses**: Sanghee Chun and Youngkhill Lee, "The Experience of Posttraumatic Growth for People with Spinal Cord Injury," *Qualitative Health Research* 18 (2008): 877–90; Alexandra Sawyer, Susan Ayers, and Andy P. Field, "Posttraumatic Growth and Adjustment Among Individuals with Cancer or HIV/AIDS: A Meta-Analysis," *Clinical Psychology Review* 30 (2010): 436–47.

79   **more than half the people who experience**: Richard G. Tedeschi and Lawrence G. Calhoun, "The Posttraumatic Growth Inventory: Measuring the Positive Legacy of Trauma," *Journal of Traumatic Stress* 9 (1996): 455–71.

79   **less than 15 percent who develop PTSD**: National Center for PTSD, U.S. Department of Veterans Affairs, "How Common Is PTSD?," calculated from the statistics presented in the report, accessed on December 14, 2016: www.ptsd.va.gov/public/PTSD-overview/basics/how-common-is-ptsd.asp.

79   **"what does not kill me makes me stronger"**: Friedrich Nietzsche, *Twilight of the Idols,* trans. R. J. Hollingdale (New York: Penguin, 1889/1977).

79   **"I am more vulnerable"**: Lawrence G. Calhoun and Richard G. Tedeschi, *Handbook of Posttraumatic Growth: Research and Practice* (New York: Routledge, 2014).

83 After loss, the emptiness of birthdays: Camille B. Wortman, "Posttraumatic Growth: Progress and Problems," *Psychological Inquiry* 15 (2004): 81–90.

84 people were asked to write and deliver: Martin E. P. Seligman, Tracy A. Steen, Nansook Park, and Christopher Peterson, "Positive Psychology Progress: Empirical Validation of Interventions," *American Psychologist* 60 (2005): 410–21. See also Fabian Gander, René T. Proyer, Willibald Ruch, and Tobias Wyss, "Strength-Based Positive Interventions: Further Evidence for Their Potential in Enhancing Well-Being and Alleviating Depression," *Journal of Happiness Studies* 14 (2013): 1241–59.

85 Many survivors of sexual abuse and assault: Patricia Frazier, Amy Conlon, and Theresa Glaser, "Positive and Negative Life Changes Following Sexual Assault," *Journal of Consulting and Clinical Psychology* 69 (2001): 1048–55; J. Curtis McMillen, Susan Zuravin, and Gregory Rideout, "Perceived Benefit from Childhood Sexual Abuse," *Journal of Consulting and Clinical Psychology* 63 (1995): 1037–43.

85 After losing a child: Darrin R. Lehman, Camille B. Wortman, and Allan F. Williams, "Long-Term Effects of Losing a Spouse or Child in a Motor Vehicle Crash," *Journal of Personality and Social Psychology* 52 (1987): 218–31.

85 Soldiers who experience significant losses: Glen H. Elder Jr. and Elizabeth Colerick Clipp, "Wartime Losses and Social Bonding: Influence Across 40 Years in Men's Lives," *Psychiatry* 51 (1988): 177–98; Glen H. Elder Jr. and Elizabeth Colerick Clipp, "Combat Experience and Emotional Health: Impairment and Resilience in Later Life," *Journal of Personality* 57 (1989): 311–41.

85 Many breast cancer survivors report: Matthew J. Cordova, Lauren L. C. Cunningham, Charles R. Carlson, and Michael A. Andrykowski, "Posttraumatic Growth Following Breast Cancer: A Controlled Comparison Study," *Health Psychology* 20 (2001): 176–85; Sharon Manne, Jamie Ostroff, Gary Winkel, et al., "Posttraumatic Growth After Breast Cancer: Patient, Partner, and Couple Perspectives," *Psychosomatic Medicine* 66 (2004): 442–54; Tzipi Weiss, "Posttraumatic Growth in Women with Breast Cancer and Their Husbands: An Intersubjective Validation Study," *Journal of Psychosocial Orthopsychiatry* 20 (2002): 65–80; Keith M. Bellizzi and Thomas O. Blank, "Predicting Posttraumatic Growth in Breast Cancer Survivors," *Health Psychology* 25 (2006): 47–56.

86 "In some way, suffering ceases to be": Frankl, *Man's Search for Meaning.*

87 Traumatic experiences can lead to deeper faith: Annick Shaw, Stephen Joseph, and P. Alex Linley, "Religion, Spirituality, and Posttraumatic Growth: A Systematic Review," *Mental Health, Religion and Culture* 8 (2005): 1–11.

87 I read an open letter: Vernon Turner, "Letter to My Younger Self," *The Players' Tribune,* May 3, 2016: www.theplayerstribune.com/vernon -turner-nfl-letter-to-my-younger-self/.

88 Family and religion are the greatest sources: Paul T. P. Wong, *The Human Quest for Meaning: Theories, Research, and Applications* (New York: Routledge, 2013); Jochen I. Menges, Danielle V. Tussing, Andreas Wihler,

and Adam Grant, "When Job Performance Is All Relative: How Family Motivation Energizes Effort and Compensates for Intrinsic Motivation," *Academy of Management Journal* (in press): http://amj.aom.org/content /early/2016/02/25/amj.2014.0898.short.

88 **The jobs where people find the most meaning**: Brent D. Rosso, Kathryn H. Dekas, and Amy Wrzesniewski, "On the Meaning of Work: A Theoretical Integration and Review," *Research in Organizational Behavior* 30 (2010): 91–127; Adam M. Grant, "The Significance of Task Significance: Job Performance Effects, Relational Mechanisms, and Boundary Conditions," *Journal of Applied Psychology* 93 (2008): 108–24; Adam M. Grant, "Relational Job Design and the Motivation to Make a Prosocial Difference," *Academy of Management Review* 32 (2007): 393–417; Adam M. Grant, "Leading with Meaning: Beneficiary Contact, Prosocial Impact, and the Performance Effects of Transformational Leadership," *Academy of Management Journal* 55 (2012): 458–76; Yitzhak Fried and Gerald R. Ferriss, "The Validity of the Job Characteristics Model: A Review and Meta-Analysis," *Personnel Psychology* 40 (1987): 287–322; PayScale, "The Most and Least Meaningful Jobs," accessed on December 14, 2016: www.pay scale.com/data-packages/most-and-least-meaningful-jobs/.

88 **meaningful work buffers against burnout**: Adam M. Grant and Sabine Sonnentag, "Doing Good Buffers Against Feeling Bad: Prosocial Impact Compensates for Negative Task and Self-Evaluations," *Organizational Behavior and Human Decision Processes* 111 (2010): 13–22; Adam M. Grant and Elizabeth M. Campbell, "Doing Good, Doing Harm, Being Well and Burning Out: The Interactions of Perceived Prosocial and Antisocial Impact in Service Work," *Journal of Occupational and Organizational Psychology* 80 (2007): 665–91. See also Thomas W. Britt, James M. Dickinson, DeWayne Moore, et al., "Correlates and Consequences of Morale Versus Depression Under Stressful Conditions," *Journal of Occupational Health Psychology* 12 (2007): 34–47; Stephen E. Humphrey, Jennifer D. Nahrgang, and Frederick P. Morgeson, "Integrating Motivational, Social, and Contextual Work Design Features: A Meta-Analytic Summary and Theoretical Extension of the Work Design Literature," *Journal of Applied Psychology* 92 (2007): 1332–56.

89 **And on days when people think**: Sabine Sonnentag and Adam M. Grant, "Doing Good at Work Feels Good at Home, but Not Right Away: When and Why Perceived Prosocial Impact Predicts Positive Affect," *Personnel Psychology* 65 (2012): 495–530.

90 **Applications to Teach for America tripled**: Abby Goodnough, "More Applicants Answer the Call for Teaching Jobs," *The New York Times,* February 11, 2002: www.nytimes.com/learning/students/pop/20020212snap tuesday.html.

90 **Before the attacks, work**: Amy Wrzesniewski, "It's Not Just a Job: Shifting Meanings of Work in the Wake of 9/11," *Journal of Management Inquiry* 11 (2002): 230–34.

90 **People were also more likely to find meaning**: J. Curtis McMillen, Elizabeth M. Smith, and Rachel H. Fisher, "Perceived Benefit and Mental Health After Three Types of Disaster," *Journal of Consulting and Clinical Psychology* 65 (1997): 733–39.

91 **After being reminded of:** Philip J. Cozzolino, Angela Dawn Staples, Law-
    rence S. Meyers, and Jamie Samboceti, "Greed, Death, and Values: From
    Terror Management to Transcendence Management Theory," *Personality
    and Social Psychology Bulletin* 30 (2004): 278–92; Adam M. Grant and Kim-
    berly Wade-Benzoni, "The Hot and Cool of Death Awareness at Work:
    Mortality Cues, Aging, and Self-Protective and Prosocial Motivations,"
    Academy of Management Review 34 (2009): 600–22.

91 **Caring for loved ones who are sick:** Robin K. Yabroff, "Financial Hard-
    ship Associated with Cancer in the United States: Findings from a
    Population-Based Sample of Adult Cancer Survivors," *Journal of Clinical
    Oncology* 34 (2016): 259–67; Echo L. Warner, Anne C. Kirchhoff, Gina E.
    Nam, and Mark Fluchel, "Financial Burden of Pediatric Cancer Patients
    and Their Families," *Journal of Oncology Practice* 11 (2015): 12–18.

91 **almost three million Americans are caring:** National Alliance for Can-
    cer Caregiving, "Cancer Caregiving in the U.S.: An Intense, Episodic,
    and Challenging Care Experience," June 2016, accessed on Decem-
    ber 18, 2016: www.caregiving.org/wp-content/uploads/2016/06/Cancer
    CaregivingReport_FINAL_June-17-2016.pdf; Alison Snyder, "How Can-
    cer in the Family Reverberates Through the Workplace," *The Wash-
    ington Post,* December 11, 2016: www.washingtonpost.com/national
    /health-science/how-cancer-in-the-family-reverberates-through-the-work
    place/2016/12/09/08311ea4-bb24-11e6-94ac-3d324840106c_story.html.

91 **Illness is a factor:** David U. Himmelstein, Deborah Thorne, Elizabeth
    Warren, and Steffie Woolhandler, "Medical Bankruptcy in the United
    States, 2007: Results of a National Study," *The American Journal of Medicine*
    122 (2009): 741–46.

91 **people with cancer are more than 2.5 times:** Scott Ramsey, David
    Blough, Anne Kirchhoff, et al., "Washington State Cancer Patients Found
    to Be at Greater Risk for Bankruptcy than People Without a Cancer Diag-
    nosis," *Health Affairs* 32 (2013): 1143–52. See also Robin Yabroff, Emily C.
    Dowling, Gery P. Guy, et al., "Financial Hardship Associated with Cancer
    in the United States: Findings from a Population-Based Sample of Adult
    Cancer Survivors," *Journal of Clinical Oncology* 34 (2015): 259–67.

91 **46 percent of Americans are unable:** Board of Governors of the Federal
    Reserve System, "Report on the Economic Well-Being of U.S. House-
    holds in 2015," May 2016, accessed on December 14, 2016: www.federal
    reserve.gov/2015-report-economic-well-being-us-households-201605.pdf.

91 **Tragedy does more than rip away:** Sally Maitlis, "Who Am I Now?
    Sensemaking and Identity in Posttraumatic Growth," in *Exploring Positive
    Identities and Organizations: Building a Theoretical and Research Foundation,*
    ed. Laura Morgan Roberts and Jane E. Dutton (New York: Psychology
    Press, 2009).

91 **Our possible selves:** Hazel Markus and Paula Nurius, "Possible Selves,"
    American Psychologist 41 (1986): 954–69; Elizabeth A. Penland, William G.
    Masten, Paul Zelhart, et al., "Possible Selves, Depression and Coping
    Skills in University Students," *Personality and Individual Differences* 29
    (2000): 963–69; Daphna Oyserman and Hazel Rose Markus, "Possible
    Selves and Delinquency," *Journal of Personality and Social Psychology* 59

(1990): 112–25; Chris Feudtner, "Hope and the Prospects of Healing at the End of Life," *The Journal of Alternative and Complementary Medicine* 11 (2005): S-23–S-30.

92 **"When one door of happiness closes"**: Helen Keller, *We Bereaved* (New York: Leslie Fulenwider Inc., 1929), accessed on December 29, 2016: https://archive.org/stream/webereavedoohele#page/22/mode/2up.

92 **many trauma survivors end up helping**: Trenton A. Williams and Dean A. Shepherd, "Victim Entrepreneurs Doing Well by Doing Good: Venture Creation and Well-Being in the Aftermath of a Resource Shock," *Journal of Business Venturing* 31 (2016): 365–87.

93 **"Every new beginning comes"**: Attributed to Lucius Annaeus Seneca; Semisonic, "Closing Time," *Feeling Strangely Fine* (MCA, 1998).

93 **"I do believe I have been changed"**: Stephen Schwartz, *Wicked*, original Broadway cast recording (Decca Broadway, 2003).

6. TAKING BACK JOY

96 **When people lose a loved one**: Margaret Shandor Miles and Alice Sterner Demi, "A Comparison of Guilt in Bereaved Parents Whose Children Died by Suicide, Accident, or Chronic Disease," *OMEGA: Journal of Death and Dying* 24 (1992): 203–15.

97 **When a company lays off employees**: Joel Brockner, Jeff Greenberg, Audrey Brockner, et al., "Layoffs, Equity Theory, and Work Performance: Further Evidence of the Impact of Survivor Guilt," *Academy of Management Journal* 29 (1986): 373–84; Barbara Kiviat, "After Layoffs, There's Survivor Guilt," *Time*, February 1, 2009: http://content.time.com/time/business/article/0,8599,1874592,00.html.

97 **A life chasing pleasure without meaning**: Roy F. Baumeister, Kathleen D. Vohs, Jennifer L. Aaker, and Emily N. Garbinsky, "Some Key Differences Between a Happy Life and a Meaningful Life," *The Journal of Positive Psychology* 8 (2013): 505–16.

97 **When we focus on others, we find**: Adam M. Grant, Elizabeth M. Campbell, Grace Chen, et al., "Impact and the Art of Motivation Maintenance: The Effects of Contact with Beneficiaries on Persistence Behavior," *Organizational Behavior and Human Decision Processes* 103 (2007): 53–67; Adam M. Grant, "Does Intrinsic Motivation Fuel the Prosocial Fire? Motivational Synergy in Predicting Persistence, Performance, and Productivity," *Journal of Applied Psychology* 93 (2008): 48–58; Nicola Bellé, "Experimental Evidence on the Relationship Between Public Service Motivation and Job Performance," *Public Administration Review* 73 (2013): 143–53.

99 **"Joy is the ultimate act of defiance"**: Bono, quoted in Brian Boyd, "Bono: The Voice of Innocence and Experience," *The Irish Times*, September 18, 2015: www.irishtimes.com/culture/music/bono-the-voice-of-innocence-and-experience-1.2355501; quote changed from "an act of defiance" to "the ultimate act of defiance" with permission.

100 **But happiness is the frequency**: Ed Diener, Ed Sandvik, and William Pavot, "Happiness Is the Frequency, Not the Intensity, of Positive Versus

Negative Affect," in *Subjective Well-Being: An Interdisciplinary Perspective*, ed. Fritz Strack, Michael Argyle, and Norbert Schwartz (New York: Pergamon, 1991).

100 **In a twelve-year study of bereaved spouses**: Frank J. Infurna and Suniya S. Luthar, "The Multidimensional Nature of Resilience to Spousal Loss," *Journal of Personality and Social Psychology* (in press): http://psycnet .apa.org/psycinfo/2016-33916-001/.

100 **"How we spend our days"**: Annie Dillard, *The Writing Life* (New York: Harper & Row, 1989).

100 **happiness is the joy you find**: Tim Urban, "How to Pick Your Life Partner—Part 2," *Wait but Why*, February 2014: http://waitbutwhy.com /2014/02/pick-life-partner-part-2.html.

101 **we are wired to focus on the negatives**: Paul Rozin and Edward B. Royzman, "Negativity Bias, Negativity Dominance, and Contagion," *Personality and Social Psychology Review* 5 (2001): 296–320; Roy F. Baumeister, Ellen Bratslavsky, Catrin Finkenauer, and Kathleen D. Vohs, "Bad Is Stronger than Good," *Review of General Psychology* 5 (2001): 323–70.

102 **But today we give that attention**: Anita DeLongis, James C. Coyne, Gayle Dakof, et al., "Relationship of Daily Hassles, Uplifts, and Major Life Events to Health Status," *Health Psychology* 1 (1982): 119–36; Vivian Kraaij, Ella Arensman, and Philip Spinhoven, "Negative Life Events and Depression in Elderly Persons: A Meta-Analysis," *The Journals of Gerontology Series B* 57 (2002): 87–94.

102 **Just as labeling negative emotions**: Michele M. Tugade, Barbara L. Fredrickson, and Lisa Feldman Barrett, "Psychological Resilience and Positive Emotional Granularity: Examining the Benefits of Positive Emotions on Coping and Health," *Journal of Personality* 72 (2004): 1161–90.

102 **Writing about joyful experiences**: Chad M. Burton and Laura A. King, "The Health Benefits of Writing About Intensely Positive Experiences," *Journal of Research in Personality* 38 (2004): 150–63; Joyce E. Bono, Theresa M. Glomb, Winny Shen, et al., "Building Positive Resources: Effects of Positive Events and Positive Reflection on Work Stress and Health," *Academy of Management Journal* 56 (2013): 1601–27.

102 **We can savor the smallest of daily events**: Anthony D. Ong, C. S. Bergeman, Toni L. Bisconti, and Kimberly A. Wallace, "Psychological Resilience, Positive Emotions, and Successful Adaptation to Stress in Later Life," *Journal of Personality and Social Psychology* 91 (2006): 730–49.

102 **As we get older, we define happiness**: Cassie Mogilner, Sepandar D. Kamvar, and Jennifer Aaker, "The Shifting Meaning of Happiness," *Social Psychological and Personality Science* 2 (2011): 395–402.

102 **"Peace is joy at rest"**: Reverend Veronica Goines, quoted in Anne Lamott, *Plan B: Further Thoughts on Faith* (New York: Riverhead, 2006); Robert Lee Hill, *The Color of Sabbath: Proclamations and Prayers for New Beginnings* (Pasadena: Hope Publishing House, 2007).

102 **Sharing positive events with another person**: Shelly L. Gable, Harry T. Reis, Emily A. Impett, and Evan R. Asher, "What Do You Do When Things Go Right? The Intrapersonal and Interpersonal Benefits of Sharing Positive Events," *Journal of Personality and Social Psychology* 87 (2004): 228–45.

102 "Joy is a discipline": Shannon Sedgwick Davis, "Joy Is a Discipline," *To My Boys*, May 18, 2014: www.2myboys.com/joy-discipline.

103 "**just manageable difficulty**": Nicholas Hobbs, "The Psychologist as Administrator," *Journal of Clinical Psychology* 25 (1959): 237–40; John Habel, "Precipitating Myself into Just Manageable Difficulties: Constructing an Intellectual Biography of Nicholas Hobbs," in *Inside Stories: Qualitative Research Reflections*, ed. Kathleen B. deMarrais (Mahwah, NJ: Erlbaum, 1998).

103 **flow**: Mihaly Csikszentmihalyi, *Finding Flow: The Psychology of Engagement with Everyday Life* (New York: Basic Books, 1998); Ryan W. Quinn, "Flow in Knowledge Work: High Performance Experience in the Design of National Security Technology," *Administrative Science Quarterly* 50 (2005): 610–41.

103 "**if Bruce Wayne watched his parents murdered**": Quoted in Jason Zinoman, "Patton Oswalt: 'I'll Never Be at 100 Percent Again,'" *The New York Times*, October 26, 2016: www.nytimes.com/2016/10/30/arts/patton-oswalt-ill-never-be-at-100-percent-again.html?_r=0; quote changed from "cut hero" to "buff hero" with permission.

103 **The physical health effects of exercise**: Mayo Clinic Staff, "Exercise: 7 Benefits of Regular Physical Activity," Mayo Clinic, October 13, 2016: www.mayoclinic.org/healthy-lifestyle/fitness/in-depth/exercise/art-20048389.

103 **Many doctors and therapists also point to exercise**: Georgia Stahopoulou, Mark B. Powers, Angela C. Berry, et al., "Exercise Interventions for Mental Health: A Quantitative and Qualitative Review," *Clinical Psychology* 13 (2006): 179–93.

103 **For some adults over fifty who suffer**: James A. Blumenthal, Michael A. Babyak, Kathleen A. Moore, et al., "Effects of Exercise Training on Older Patients with Major Depression," *Archives of Internal Medicine* 159 (1999): 2349–56.

104 **There are more refugees today**: UNHCR, the UN Refugee Agency, "Figures at a Glance," accessed on December 18, 2016: www.unhcr.org/en-us/figures-at-a-glance.html; Scott Arbeiter, "America's Duty to Take in Refugees," *The New York Times*, September 23, 2016: www.nytimes.com/2016/09/24/opinion/americas-duty-to-take-in-refugees.html.

7. RAISING RESILIENT KIDS

106 **award-winning painter Timothy Chambers**: www.iguanaacademy.com/timothy-chambers/.

107 **Kim watched a talk Adam gave on resilience**: Adam Grant, "The Surprising Habits of Original Thinkers," TED, April 2016: www.ted.com/talks/adam_grant_the_surprising_habits_of_original_thinkers.

110 **one in six in Australia**: Australian Council of Social Service, "Poverty in Australia 2014," accessed on March 11, 2017: www.acoss.org.au/images/uploads/ACOSS_Poverty_in_Australia_2014.pdf.

110 **one in five in the U.K.**: Feargal McGuinness, "House of Commons Briefing Paper: Poverty in the UK: Statistics," accessed on March 11, 2017:

http://researchbriefings.parliament.uk/ResearchBriefing/Summary/
SN07096#fullreport.

110 **three in five in South Africa**: Monde Makiwane, Mzikazi Nduna and
Nene Ernest Khalema, *Children in South African Families: Lives and Times*
(Cambridge Scholars Publishing: 2016).

110 **one-third of black**: National Poverty Center, "Poverty in the United
States," accessed on December 14, 2016: www.npc.umich.edu/poverty/.

110 **Forty-three percent of children of single mothers**: Bernadette D. Proc-
tor, Jessica L. Semega, and Melissa A. Kollar, "Income and Poverty in the
United States: 2015," United States Census Bureau, September 2016: www
.census.gov/content/dam/Census/library/publications/2016/demo
/p60-256.pdf.

110 **More than two and a half million children**: Katie Reilly, "Sesame Street
Reaches Out to 2.7 Million American Children with an Incarcerated Parent," Pew Research Center, June 21, 2013: www.pewresearch.org/fact
-tank/2013/06/21/sesame-street-reaches-out-to-2-7-million-american
-children-with-an-incarcerated-parent.

110 **These extreme levels of harm and deprivation**: Katie A. McLaughlin
and Margaret A. Sheridan, "Beyond Cumulative Risk: A Dimensional
Approach to Childhood Adversity," *Current Directions in Psychological Science* 25 (2016): 239–45.

110 **High-quality preschool education**: Gregory Camilli, Sadako Vargas,
Sharon Ryan, and William Steven Barnett, "Meta-Analysis of the Effects
of Early Education Interventions on Cognitive and Social Development,"
Teachers College Record 122 (2010): 579–620.

110 **the Nurse-Family Partnership**: www.nursefamilypartnership.org/.

110 **When disadvantaged families are provided**: Nicholas Kristof and Sheryl
WuDunn, "The Way to Beat Poverty," *The New York Times*, September 12,
2014: www.nytimes.com/2014/09/14/opinion/sunday/nicholas-kristof
-the-way-to-beat-poverty.html.

111 **every dollar put into these visits**: Lynn A. Karoly, M. Rebecca Kilburn,
and Jill S. Cannon, "Early Childhood Interventions: Proven Results,
Future Promise," RAND Labor and Population 2005: www.rand.org
/content/dam/rand/pubs/monographs/2005/RAND_MG341.pdf.

111 **Resilience leads to greater happiness**: Ann S. Masten, "Ordinary Magic:
Resilience Processes in Development," *American Psychologist* 56 (2001):
227–38; Carolyn M. Youssef and Fred Luthans, "Positive Organizational
Behavior in the Workplace: The Impact of Hope, Optimism, and Resil-
ience," *Journal of Management* 33 (2007): 774–800; Salvatore R. Maddi,
Hardiness: Turning Stressful Circumstances into Resilient Growth (New York:
Springer Science & Business Media, 2012).

111 **It's a lifelong project**: Brian R. Little, Katariina Salmela-Aro, and Susan D.
Phillips, eds., *Personal Project Pursuit: Goals, Action, and Human Flourishing*
(Mahwah, NJ: Erlbaum, 2006).

111 **"competent, confident, and caring young adults"**: Emmy E. Werner,
"High-Risk Children in Young Adulthood: A Longitudinal Study from
Birth to 32 Years," *American Journal of Orthopsychiatry* 59 (1989): 72–81.

111 **The same holds true for children**: Mary Karapetian Alvord and Judy Johnson Grados, "Enhancing Resilience in Children: A Proactive Approach," *Professional Psychology: Research in Practice* 36 (2005): 238–45.

112 **Change Your Shoes**: Kathy Andersen started this program and made it a Lean In Circle. For more information, see https://leanincircles.org /chapter/change-your-shoes.

113 **children respond better to adversity**: Carol S. Dweck, *Mindset: The New Psychology of Success* (New York: Random House, 2006).

113 **Whether children develop a fixed or growth mindset**: Claudia M. Mueller and Carol S. Dweck, "Praise for Intelligence Can Undermine Children's Motivation and Performance," *Journal of Personality and Social Psychology* 75 (1998): 33–52.

113 **After students at risk of dropping out**: David Paunesku, Gregory M. Walton, Carissa Romero, et al., "Mind-set Interventions Are a Scalable Treatment for Academic Underachievement," *Psychological Science* 26 (2015): 784–93.

113 **When college freshmen completed**: David S. Yeager, Gregory M. Walton, Shannon T. Brady, et al., "Teaching a Lay Theory Before College Narrows Achievement Gaps at Scale," *Proceedings of the National Academy of Sciences* 113 (2016): 12111–13.

114 **Today the importance of helping kids**: Kyla Haimovitz and Carol S. Dweck, "What Predicts Children's Fixed and Growth Mind-Sets? Not Their Parents' Views of Intelligence but Their Parents' Views of Failure," *Psychological Science* 27 (2016): 859–69.

114 **"normalizing struggle"**: Julie Lythcott-Haims, *How to Raise an Adult: Break Free of the Overparenting Trap and Prepare Your Kid for Success* (New York: Holt, 2015).

114 **"Maybe math isn't one"**: Carol Dweck, "Carol Dweck Revisits the Growth Mindset," *Education Week*, September 22, 2015: www.edweek .org/ew/articles/2015/09/23/carol-dweck-revisits-the-growth-mindset .html.

114 **mattering**: Morris Rosenberg and B. Claire McCullough, "Mattering: Inferred Significance and Mental Health Among Adolescents," *Research in Community and Mental Health* 2 (1981): 163–82; Login S. George and Crystal L. Park, "Meaning in Life as Comprehension, Purpose, and Mattering: Toward Integration and New Research Questions," *Review of General Psychology* 20 (2016): 205–20.

114 **those who felt they mattered were less likely**: Gregory C. Elliott, Melissa F. Colangelo, and Richard J. Gelles, "Mattering and Suicide Ideation: Establishing and Elaborating a Relationship," *Social Psychology Quarterly* 68 (2005): 223–38.

114 **Lesbian, gay, and bisexual youths**: Laura Kann, Emily O'Malley Olsen, Tim McManus, et al., "Sexual Identity, Sex of Sexual Contacts, and Health-Risk Behaviors Among Students in Grades 9–12," Centers for Disease Control and Prevention, *Morbidity and Mortality Weekly Report*, June 10, 2011: www.cdc.gov/mmwr/pdf/ss/ss6oeo606.pdf.

116 **Klassen Time**: Jessica Alexander, "Teaching Kids Empathy: In Danish Schools, It's . . . Well, It's a Piece of Cake," *Salon*, August 9, 2016: www

.salon.com/2016/08/09/teaching-kids-empathy-in-danish-schools-its-well-its-a-piece-of-cake; Jessica Joelle Alexander and Iben Dissing Sandahl, *The Danish Way of Parenting: What the Happiest People in the World Know About Raising Confident, Capable Kids* (New York: TarcherPerigee, 2016).

116 **The children learn empathy**: Martin L. Hoffman, *Empathy and Moral Development: Implications for Caring and Justice* (New York: Cambridge University Press, 2001).

116 **a resilience program called Girls First**: http://corstone.org/girls-first -bihar-india/.

117 **she intervened to stop a boy**: Kate Leventhal, "Ritu's Story: A New Advocate for Peace and Women's Rights," CorStone, November 19, 2015: http://corstone.org/ritus-story-peace-rights/.

118 **when teachers are told students from stigmatized groups**: Lee Jussim and Kent D. Harber, "Teacher Expectations and Self-Fulfilling Prophecies: Knowns and Unknowns, Resolved and Unresolved Controversies," *Personality and Social Psychology Review* 9 (2005): 131–55; Robert Rosenthal and Lenore Jacobson, "Teachers' Expectancies: Determinants of Pupils' IQ Gains," *Psychological Reports* 19 (1966): 115–18; Monica J. Harris and Robert Rosenthal, "Mediation of Interpersonal Expectancy Effects: 31 Meta-Analyses," *Psychological Bulletin* 97 (1985): 363–86.

118 **Believe you can learn from failure**: David S. Yeager and Carol S. Dweck, "Mindsets That Promote Resilience: When Students Believe That Personal Characteristics Can Be Developed," *Educational Psychologist* 47 (2012): 302–14.

118 **Believe you matter**: Adam M. Grant and Francesca Gino, "A Little Thanks Goes a Long Way: Explaining Why Gratitude Expressions Motivate Prosocial Behavior," *Journal of Personality and Social Psychology* 98 (2010): 946–55.

119 **More than 1.8 million children in America**: Social Security Administration, "Benefits Paid by Type of Beneficiary," accessed on December 14, 2016: www.ssa.gov/oact/progdata/icp.html.

119 **in a national poll nearly three-quarters said**: "Life with Grief Research," *Comfort Zone News*, accessed on December 14, 2016: www.comfortzone camp.org/news/childhood-bereavement-study-results.

120 **kids have more neural plasticity**: Joan Stiles, "Neural Plasticity and Cognitive Development," *Developmental Neuropsychology* 18 (2000): 237–72. See also Dante Ciccheti, "Resilience Under Conditions of Extreme Stress: A Multilevel Perspective," *World Psychiatry* 9 (2010): 145–54.

120 **They have shorter "feeling spans"**: Kenneth J. Doka and Joyce D. Davidson, eds., *Living with Grief: Who We Are, How We Grieve* (New York: Routledge, 1998).

121 **When we're tired**: Christopher M. Barnes, Cristiano L. Guarana, Shazia Nauman, and Dejun Tony King, "Too Tired to Inspire or Be Inspired: Sleep Deprivation and Charismatic Leadership," *Journal of Applied Psychology* 101 (2016): 1191–99; Brett Litwiller, Lori Anderson Snyder, William D. Taylor, and Logan M. Steele, "The Relationship Between Sleep and Work: A Meta-Analysis," *Journal of Applied Psychology* (in press): http://psycnet .apa.org/psycinfo/2016-57450-001/.

121   **Girls Leadership**: https://girlsleadership.org/.

124   **When children grow up with a strong understanding**: Robyn Fivush, Jennifer Bohanek, Rachel Robertson, and Marshall Duke, "Family Narratives and the Development of Children's Emotional Well-Being," in *Family Stories and the Life Course: Across Time and Generations,* ed. Michael W. Pratt and Barbara H. Fiese (Mahwah, NJ: Erlbaum, 2004); Bruce Feiler, "The Stories That Bind Us," *The New York Times,* March 15, 2013: www .nytimes.com/2013/03/17/fashion/the-family-stories-that-bind-us-this -life.html.

124   **Giving all members of the family**: Jennifer G. Bohanek, Kelly A. Marin, Robyn Fivush, and Marshall P. Duke, "Family Narrative Interaction and Children's Sense of Self," *Family Process* 45 (2006): 39–54.

124   **Nostalgia is literally**: Constantine Sedikides, Tim Wildschut, Jamie Arndt, and Clay Routledge, "Nostalgia: Past, Present, and Future," *Current Directions in Psychological Science* 17 (2008): 304–7.

125   **a program at Arizona State University**: Rachel A. Haine, Tim S. Ayers, Irwin N. Sandler, and Sharlene A. Wolchik, "Evidence-Based Practices for Parentally Bereaved Children and Their Families," *Professional Psychology: Research and Practice* 39 (2008): 113–21. See also Margaret Stroebe and Henk Schut, "Family Matters in Bereavement: Toward an Integrative Intra-Interpersonal Coping Model," *Perspectives on Psychological Science* 10 (2015): 873–79. More details about the Family Bereavement Program are at https://reachinstitute.asu.edu/programs/family-bereavement.

125   **happiness is remembered, not just experienced**: Daniel Kahneman, *Thinking, Fast and Slow* (New York: Farrar, Straus and Giroux, 2012).

125   **Now I take videos**: Kristin Diehl, Gal Zauberman, and Alixandra Barasch, "How Taking Photos Increases Enjoyment of Experiences," *Journal of Personality and Social Psychology* 111 (2016): 119–40.

8. FINDING STRENGTH TOGETHER

127   "**We are caught in an inescapable network**": Martin Luther King Jr., "Letter from a Birmingham Jail," April 16, 1963: quoted at www.the atlantic.com/politics/archive/2013/04/martin-luther-kings-letter-from -birmingham-jail/274668/.

127   **In 1972, a plane flying**: Spencer Harrison, "The Role of Hope in Organizing: The Case of the 1972 Andes Flight Disaster" (working paper, 2016); Piers Paul Read, *Alive: The Story of the Andes Survivors* (Philadelphia: Lippincott, 1974); Nando Parrado, *Miracle in the Andes: 72 Days on the Mountain and My Long Trek Home* (New York: Crown, 2006); Roberto Canessa and Pablo Vierci, *I Had to Survive: How a Plane Crash in the Andes Inspired My Calling to Save Lives* (New York: Atria Books, 2016); Michael Useem, *The Go Point: How to Get Off the Fence by Knowing What to Do and When to Do It* (New York: Three Rivers Press, 2006); Pablo Vierci, *La Sociedad de la Nieve: Por Primera Vez Los 16 Sobrevivientes de los Andes Cuentan la Historia Completa* (Argentina: Editorial Sudamericana, 2008), translated from the Spanish by Spencer Harrison.

129 "communities of people generate new images": James D. Ludema, Timothy B. Wilmot, and Suresh Srivastava, "Organizational Hope: Reaffirming the Constructive Task of Social and Organizational Inquiry," *Human Relations* 50 (1997): 1015–52.

129 Believing in new possibilities helps people: C. R. Snyder, "Conceptualizing, Measuring, and Nurturing Hope," *Journal of Counseling and Development* 73 (1995): 355–60; C. R. Snyder, *Handbook of Hope* (San Diego: Academic Press, 2000).

129 "grounded hope": David B. Feldman and Lee Daniel Kravetz, *Supersurvivors: The Surprising Link Between Suffering and Success* (New York: Harper Wave, 2014).

129 when thirty-three miners were trapped: "Chile Miners Get Support from 'Alive' Crash Survivors," BBC News, September 4, 2010: www.bbc .com/news/world-latin-america-11190456; "'Alive' Survivors Reach Out to Trapped Chilean Miners," *Weekend Edition Sunday,* NPR, September 5, 2010: www.npr.org/templates/story/story.php?storyId=129662796; "A Survivor's Message to Miners," YouTube, accessed on December 15, 2016: www.youtube.com/watch?v=kLHhTLbjtkY.

131 Experience Camps: www.experience.camp.

132 He has since testified: "Testimony of Former SHU Inmate Steven Czifra at the Joint Legislative Hearing on Solitary Confinement in California," October 9, 2013, accessed on December 23, 2016: www.whatthefolly .com/2013/10/22/transcript-testimony-of-former-shu-inmate-steven -czifra-at-the-joint-legislative-hearing-on-solitary-confinement-in-califor nia-oct-9-2013/; "Steven Czifra Speaks on Solitary Confinement in North Berkeley," YouTube, November 6, 2013, accessed on December 23, 2016: www.youtube.com/watch?v=aodLBlt1i00.

132 Underground Scholars Initiative: Larissa MacFarquhar, "Building a Prison-to-School Pipeline," *The New Yorker,* December 12, 2016: www .newyorker.com/magazine/2016/12/12/the-ex-con-scholars-of-berkeley; Jessie Lau, "Incarceration to Convocation," *The Daily Californian,* May 10, 2015: www.dailycal.org/2015/05/10/incarceration-to-convocation/.

133 The Posse Foundation: www.possefoundation.org.

133 shared narratives can build collective resilience: Michèle Lamont, Graziella Moraes Silva, Jessica S. Welburn, et al., *Getting Respect: Responding to Stigma and Discrimination in the United States, Brazil, and Israel* (Princeton: Princeton University Press, 2016).

133 When college students were reminded: Michael Johns, Toni Schmader, and Andy Martens, "Knowing Is Half the Battle: Teaching Stereotype Threat as a Means of Improving Women's Math Performance," *Psychological Science* 16 (2005): 175–79.

134 black students scored lower: Claude M. Steele and Joshua Aronson, "Stereotype Threat and the Intellectual Test Performance of African Americans," *Journal of Personality and Social Psychology* 69 (1995): 797–811. For a review, see Hannah-Hanh D. Nguyen and Ann Marie Ryan, "Does Stereotype Threat Affect Test Performance of Minorities and Women? A Meta-Analysis of Experimental Evidence," *Journal of Applied Psychology* 93 (2008): 1314–34.

134   **"stereotype threat"**: Claude M. Steele, "A Threat in the Air: How Stereotypes Shape Intellectual Identity and Performance," *American Psychologist* 52 (1997): 613–29; Jenessa R. Shapiro and Steven L. Neuberg, "From
Stereotype Threat to Stereotype Threats: Implications of a Multi-Threat
Framework for Causes, Moderators, Mediators, Consequences, and Interventions," *Personality and Social Psychology Review* 11 (2007): 107–30.

134   **"The buzz around the school"**: Tina Rosenberg, "Beyond SATs, Finding Success in Numbers," *The New York Times*, February 15, 2012: http://
opinionator.blogs.nytimes.com/2012/02/15/beyond-sats-finding-success
-in-numbers/?scp=1&sq=fixes%20stereotype%20threat&st=cse.

134   **peer support can have a big impact**: Dan S. Chiaburu and David A. Harrison, "Do Peers Make the Place? Conceptual Synthesis and Meta-Analysis
of Coworker Effects on Perceptions, Attitudes, OCBs, and Performance,"
Journal of Applied Psychology 93 (2008): 1082–103; Chockalingam Viswes-
varan, Juan I. Sanchez, and Jeffrey Fisher, "The Role of Social Support in
the Process of Work Stress: A Meta-Analysis," *Journal of Vocational Behavior* 54 (1999): 314–34.

135   **By helping people cope with difficult circumstances**: Geoff DeVerteuil
and Oleg Golubchikov, "Can Resilience Be Redeemed?" *City: Analysis of
Urban Trends, Culture, Theory, Policy, Action* 20 (2016): 143–51; Markus Keck
and Patrick Sakdapolrak, "What Is Social Resilience? Lessons Learned
and Ways Forward," *Erdkunde* 67 (2013): 5–19.

136   **"On Friday night, you stole the life"**: Antoine Leiris, *You Will Not Have My
Hate* (New York: Penguin Press, 2016).

136   **"Moral elevation" describes the feeling**: Jonathan Haidt, "Elevation and
the Positive Psychology of Morality," in *Flourishing: Positive Psychology
and the Life Well-Lived*, ed. Corey L. M. Keyes and Jonathan Haidt (Washington, DC: American Psychological Association, 2003); Rico Pohling
and Rhett Diessner, "Moral Elevation and Moral Beauty: A Review of
the Empirical Literature," *Review of General Psychology* 20 (2016): 412–25;
Sara B. Algoe and Jonathan Haidt, "Witnessing Excellence in Action: The
'Other-Praising' Emotions of Elevation, Gratitude, and Admiration," *The
Journal of Positive Psychology* 4 (2009): 105–27; Simone Schnall, Jean Roper,
and Daniel M. T. Fessler, "Elevation Leads to Altruistic Behavior," *Psychological Science* 21 (2010): 315–20.

136   **"the better angels of our nature"**: Abraham Lincoln's first inaugural
address, March 4, 1861, accessed on December 15, 2016: http://avalon.law
.yale.edu/19th_century/lincoln1.asp.

136   **elevation leads us to look**: Dan Freeman, Karl Aquino, and Brent McFer-
ran, "Overcoming Beneficiary Race as an Impediment to Charitable
Donations: Social Dominance Orientation, the Experience of Moral
Elevation, and Donation Behavior," *Personality and Social Psychology Bul-
letin* 35 (2009): 72–84; Karl Aquino, Brent McFerran, and Marjorie Laven,
"Moral Identity and the Experience of Moral Elevation in Response to
Acts of Uncommon Goodness," *Journal of Personality and Social Psychology*
100 (2011): 703–18; Jane E. Dutton, Monica C. Worline, Peter J. Frost, and
Jacoba Lilius, "Explaining Compassion Organizing," *Administrative Sci-
ence Quarterly* 51 (2006): 59–96.

136 "Let no man pull you so low": Martin Luther King Jr., quoted in Clayborne Carson and Peter Holloran, eds., *A Knock at Midnight: Inspiration from the Great Sermons of Reverend Martin Luther King, Jr.* (New York: Grand Central, 2000).

136 Emanuel African Methodist Episcopal Church in Charleston: Elahe Izadi, "The Powerful Words of Forgiveness Delivered to Dylann Roof by Victims' Relatives," *The Washington Post*, June 19, 2015: www.washington post.com/news/post-nation/wp/2015/06/19/hate-wont-win-the-power ful-words-delivered-to-dylann-roof-by-victims-relatives; John Eligon and Richard Fausset, "Defiant Show of Unity in Charleston Church That Lost 9 to Racist Violence," *The New York Times*, June 21, 2015: www .nytimes.com/2015/06/22/us/ame-church-in-charleston-reopens-as -congregation-mourns-shooting-victims.html; Alexis Simmons, "Families Impacted by Gun Violence Unite at Mother Emanuel Calling for Gun Reform," *KCTV News*, April 24, 2016: www.kctv5.com/story/31804155 /families-impacted-by-gun-violence-unite-at-mother-emanuel-calling -for-gun-reform; Michael S. Schmidt, "Background Check Flaw Let Dylann Roof Buy Gun, F.B.I. Says," *The New York Times*, July 10, 2015: www.nytimes.com/2015/07/11/us/background-check-flaw-let-dylann -roof-buy-gun-fbi-says.html.

137 led the congregation in singing "Amazing Grace": "President Obama Sings 'Amazing Grace,'" YouTube, accessed on January 13, 2017: www .youtube.com/watch?v=IN05jVNBs64.

137 "What unites us is stronger": Richard Fausset and John Eligon, "Charleston Church Reopens in Moving Service as Congregation Mourns," *The Charlotte Observer*, June 21, 2015: www.charlotteobserver.com/news/local /article25113397.html.

138 the Charleston Area Justice Ministry: http://thedartcenter.org/.

138 In 2010 alone, there were approximately four hundred: Dean A. Shepherd and Trenton A. Williams, "Local Venturing as Compassion Organizing in the Aftermath of a Natural Disaster: The Role of Localness and Community in Reducing Suffering," *Journal of Management Studies* 51 (2014): 952–94.

139 Resilient communities have strong social ties: See Daniel P. Aldrich and Michelle A. Meyer, "Social Capital and Community Resilience," *American Behavioral Scientist* 59 (2015): 254–69; Stevan E. Hobfoll, Patricia Watson, Carl C. Bell, et al., "Five Essential Elements of Immediate and Mid-Term Mass Trauma Intervention: Empirical Evidence," *Psychiatry* 70 (2007): 283–315. Communities that have more financial resources are often more resilient too. After Hurricane Andrew hit Florida in August 1992, people were significantly more likely to develop PTSD if they lost their homes and could not obtain the funding to rebuild: Gail Ironson, Christina Wynings, Neil Schneiderman, et al., "Posttraumatic Stress Symptoms, Intrusive Thoughts, Loss, and Immune Function After Hurricane Andrew," *Psychosomatic Medicine* 59 (1997): 128–41. And psychologists note that "moves by the state of Mississippi to force insurance companies to pay for damages following state law is a critical mental health intervention": Hobfoll et al., "Five Essential Elements of Immediate and Mid-Term Mass Trauma Intervention."

139   **After the 1994 genocide in Rwanda**: J. P. De Jong, Wilma F. Scholte, Maarten Koeter, and Augustinus A. M. Hart, "The Prevalence of Mental Health Problems in Rwandan and Burundese Refugee Camps," *Acta Psychiatrica Scandinavica* 102 (2000): 171–77.

139   **The camps with the greatest resilience**: Joop de Jong, ed., *Trauma, War, and Violence: Public Mental Health in Socio-Cultural Context* (New York: Springer, 2002).

140   **"leftover women"**: Brooke Larmer, "The Price of Marriage in China," *The New York Times*, March 9, 2013: www.nytimes.com/2013/03/10/business/in-a-changing-china-new-matchmaking-markets.html; A.A., "'Leftover' and Proud," *The Economist*, August 1, 2014: www.economist.com/blogs/analects/2014/08/womens-voices.

140   **"absolutely nothing until she is married"**: Clarissa Sebag-Montefiore, "Romance with Chinese Characteristics," *The New York Times*, August 21, 2012: http://latitude.blogs.nytimes.com/2012/08/21/romance-with-chinese-characteristics/?_r=0.

140   **More than 80,000 women**: Jenni Risku, "Reward Actors Who Promote Diversity: Lean In China's Virginia Tan," *e27*, September 19, 2016: https://e27.co/reward-actors-who-promote-diversity-lean-in-chinas-virginia-tan-20160916/.

9.   FAILING AND LEARNING AT WORK

143   **whether a space flight will succeed**: Peter M. Madsen and Vinit Desai, "Failing to Learn? The Effects of Failure and Success on Organizational Learning in the Global Orbital Launch Vehicle Industry," *Academy of Management Journal* 53 (2010): 451–76.

144   **Just as all people need resilience**: Trenton A. Williams, Daniel A. Gruber, Kathleen M. Sutcliffe, et al., "Organizational Response to Adversity: Fusing Crisis Management and Resilience Research Streams," *Academy of Management Annals* (in press).

144   **companies that kept going**: Edie Lutnick, *An Unbroken Bond: The Untold Story of How the 658 Cantor Fitzgerald Families Faced the Tragedy of 9/11 and Beyond* (New York: Emergence Press, 2011).

145   **this chalkboard was put up**: "We Asked People to Tell Us Their Biggest Regrets—But What They All Had in Common Was Heartbreaking," *A Plus*, January 22, 2016: http://aplus.com/a/clean-slate-blackboard-experiment.

145   **we usually regret the chances we missed**: Thomas Gilovich and Victoria Husted Medvec, "The Experience of Regret: What, When, and Why," *Psychological Review* 102 (1995): 379–95.

147   **morbidity and mortality conferences**: Patrice François, Frédéric Prate, Gwenaëlle Vidal-Trecan, et al., "Characteristics of Morbidity and Mortality Conferences Associated with the Implementation of Patient Safety Improvement Initiatives, An Observational Study," *BMC Health Services Research* 16 (2015), http://bmchealthservres.biomedcentral.com

/articles/10.1186/s12916-016-1279-8; Juliet Higginson, Rhiannon Walters, and Naomi Fulop, "Mortality and Morbidity Meetings: An Untapped Resource for Improving the Governance of Patient Safety?" *BMJ Quality and Safety* 21 (2012): 1–10.

147   **When it's safe to talk about mistakes**: Amy C. Edmondson, "Learning from Mistakes Is Easier Said Than Done: Group and Organizational Influences on the Detection and Correction of Human Error," *The Journal of Applied Behavioral Science* 32 (1996): 5–28.

147   **more honest in their CVs**: Melanie Stefan, "A CV of Failures," *Nature* 468 (2010): 467; Johannes Haushofer CV, accessed on December 15, 2016: www.princeton.edu/~joha.

148   **Kind Design**: Jack Deming, "Native Son Suffers Loss from Western Mountain Flooding," *The Deerfield Valley News*, 2013: www.dvalnews .com/view/full_story_obits/23695561/article-Native-son-suffers-loss -from-western-mountain-flooding.

148   **Teams that focus on learning from failure**: Cathy van Dyck, Michael Frese, Markus Baer, and Sabine Sonnentag, "Organizational Error Management Culture and Its Impact on Performance: A Two-Study Replication," *Journal of Applied Psychology* 90 (2005): 1228–40.

149   **although fishing for compliments hurts**: Susan J. Ashford, Ruth Blatt, and Don VandeWalle, "Reflections on the Looking Glass: A Review of Research on Feedback-Seeking Behavior in Organizations," *Journal of Management* 29 (2003): 773–99. Many people hesitate to ask for feedback, worrying the information will highlight their weaknesses. These fears are unfounded: asking for criticism typically leads to more positive evaluations from supervisors, subordinates, and peers.

149   **Adam became Wharton's top-rated professor**: https://mba-inside .wharton.upenn.edu/class-of-1984-awardees/ and https://mba-inside .wharton.upenn.edu/excellence-in-teaching-class-of-1984-awards.

150   **"Top athletes and singers have coaches"**: Atul Gawande, "The Coach in the Operating Room," *The New Yorker*, October 3, 2011: www.newyorker .com/magazine/2011/10/03/personal-best.

150   **"The measure of who we are"**: Gregg Popovich, quoted in J. A. Adande, "Spurs' Fortitude Fueled Title Run," ESPN, November 19, 2014: www .espn.com/nba/story/_/id/11901128/spurs-2014-title-run-started-game -7-2013-finals.

150   **"We will always spend more than half"**: Theo Epstein, quoted in Bill Pennington, "Cubs' Theo Epstein Is Making Lightning Strike Twice," *The New York Times*, September 29, 2016: www.nytimes.com/2016/10/02/sports/ baseball/theo-epstein-chicago-cubs-boston-red-sox-world-series.html.

151   **"After every low score you receive"**: Douglas Stone and Sheila Heen, *Thanks for the Feedback: The Science and Art of Receiving Feedback Well* (New York: Viking, 2014).

152   **a single sentence can make people more open**: David S. Yeager, Valerie Purdie-Vaughns, Julio Garcia, et al., "Breaking the Cycle of Mistrust: Wise Interventions to Provide Critical Feedback Across the Racial Divide," *Journal of Experimental Psychology: General* 143 (2014): 804–24.

10. TO LOVE AND LAUGH AGAIN

160 **getting married increased average happiness only**: Richard E. Lucas,
     Andrew E. Clark, Yannis Georgellis, and Ed Diener, "Reexamining Adap-
     tation and the Set Point Model of Happiness: Reactions to Changes in
     Marital Status," *Journal of Personality and Social Psychology* 84 (2003): 527–39.
     Meanwhile, couples who ended up divorcing were already becoming less
     happy as the wedding approached and their happiness climbed after the
     divorce.

160 **people who choose to be single**: Richard E. Lucas and Portia S. Dyren-
     forth, "The Myth of Marital Bliss?" *Psychological Inquiry* 16 (2005): 111–15;
     Maike Luhmann, Wilhelm Hofmann, Michael Eid, and Richard E. Lucas,
     "Subjective Well-Being and Adaptation to Life Events: A Meta-Analysis,"
     Journal of Personality and Social Psychology 102 (2012): 592–615.

160 **"Singles are stereotyped"**: Bella DePaulo, *Singled Out: How Singles Are
     Stereotyped, Stigmatized, and Ignored, and Still Live Happily Ever After* (New
     York: St. Martin's Press, 2006).

161 **"Blame me if you like"**: Aaron Ben-Zeév, "Love After Death: The
     Widows' Romantic Predicaments," The Center for Behavioral Health,
     April 12, 2012: www.njpsychologist.com/blog/love-after-death-the-widows
     -romantic-predicaments/.

161 **after a partner dies, men are more likely**: Deborah Carr, "The Desire to
     Date and Remarry Among Older Widows and Widowers," *Journal of Mar-
     riage and Family* 66 (2004): 1051–68; Danielle S. Schneider, Paul A. Sledge,
     Stephen R. Schuchter, and Sidney Zisook, "Dating and Remarriage over
     the First Two Years of Widowhood," *Annals of Clinical Psychiatry* 8 (1996):
     51–57; Karin Wolff and Camille B. Wortman, "Psychological Conse-
     quences of Spousal Loss Among Older Adults," in *Spousal Bereavement in
     Late Life*, ed. Deborah S. Carr, Randolph M. Nesse, and Camille B. Wort-
     man (New York: Springer, 2005).

162 **In the U.K.**: John Haskey, "Divorce and Remarriage in England
     and Wales," accessed on March 11, 2017 at: www.ons.gov.uk/ons/
     rel/population-trends-rd/population-trends/no--95--spring-1999/
     divorce-and-remarriage-in-england-and-wales.pdf?format=hi-vis.

162 **And in India**: Martha Alter Chen, *Perpetual Mourning: Widowhood in Rural
     India* (Oxford University Press, 2000).

162 **In some parts of India**: Nilanjana Bhowmick, "If You're an Indian
     Widow, Your Children Could Kick You Out and Take Everything," *Time*,
     October 7, 2013: http://world.time.com/2013/10/07/if-youre-an-indian
     -widow-your-children-could-kick-you-out-and-take-everything/.

162 **In some Nigerian villages**: Osai Ojigho, "Scrape Her Head and Lay Her
     Bare: Widowhood Practices and Culture," *Gender Across Borders*, Octo-
     ber 28, 2011: www.genderacrossborders.com/2011/10/28/scrape-her-head
     -and-lay-her-bare-widowhood-practices-and-culture/.

163 **Discrimination against widows has been observed**: Haider Rizvi,
     "RIGHTS: Mistreatment of Widows a Poorly Kept Secret," IPS, June 23,
     2008: www.ipsnews.net/2008/06/rights-mistreatment-of-widows-a-poorly
     -kept-secret/.

163 **In many countries, widows have difficulty**: Mary Kimani, "Women Struggle to Secure Land Rights," *Africa Renewal,* April 2008: www.un.org /africarenewal/magazine/april-2008/women-struggle-secure-land -rights; UN Women, "Empowering Widows: An Overview of Policies and Programs in India, Nepal and Sri Lanka," accessed on December 15, 2016: www2.unwomen.org/~/media/field%20office%20eseasia/docs /publications/2015/09/final_empowering%20widows_report%202014 .pdf?v=1&d=20150908T104700.

164 **a blog by author Abel Keogh**: www.abelkeogh.com/blog.

165 **Brain scans of people in love**: See Arthur Aron, Helen Fisher, Debra J. Mashek, et al., "Reward, Motivation, and Emotion Systems Associated with Early-Stage Intense Romantic Love," *Journal of Neurophysiology* 94 (2005): 327–37; Helen Fisher, Arthur Aron, and Lucy L. Brown, "Romantic Love: An fMRI Study of a Neural Mechanism for Mate Choice," *The Journal of Comparative Neurology* 493 (2005): 58–62.

165 **After we fall in love**: Arthur Aron, Meg Paris, and Elaine N. Aron, "Falling in Love: Prospective Studies of Self-Concept Change," *Journal of Personality and Social Psychology* 69 (1995): 1102–12; Elaine N. Aron and Arthur Aron, "Love and the Expansion of the Self: The State of the Model," *Personal Relationships* 3 (1996): 45–58.

166 **Surgery patients who watch comedies**: James Rotton and Mark Shats, "Effects of State Humor, Expectancies, and Choice on Postsurgical Mood and Self-Medication: A Field Experiment," *Journal of Applied Social Psychology* 26 (1996): 1775–94. This was the case when they had learned about health benefits of humor and got to choose their film.

166 **Soldiers who make jokes**: Smadar Bizi, Giora Keinan, and Benjamin Beit-Hallahmi, "Humor and Coping with Stress: A Test Under Real-Life Conditions," *Personality and Individual Differences* 9 (1988): 951–56.

167 **People who laugh naturally**: Dacher Keltner and George A. Bonanno, "A Study of Laughter and Dissociation: Distinct Correlates of Laughter and Smiling During Bereavement," *Journal of Personality and Social Psychology* 73 (1997): 687–702.

167 **Couples who laugh together**: John Mordechai Gottman and Robert Wayne Levenson, "The Timing of Divorce: Predicting When a Couple Will Divorce over a 14-Year Period," *Journal of Marriage and Family* 62 (2000): 737–45.

167 **humor lowers our heart rate**: Michelle Gayle Newman and Arthur A. Stone, "Does Humor Moderate the Effects of Experimentally-Induced Stress?" *Annals of Behavioral Medicine* 18 (1996): 101–9.

167 **"if you can reduce them to ridicule"**: Mel Brooks, quoted in Forrest Wickman, "Watch the New Documentary About Mel Brooks," *Slate,* May 28, 2013: www.slate.com/blogs/browbeat/2013/05/28/_mel_brooks _make_a_noise_the_pbs_american_masters_documentary_is_now _available.html.

167 **Jokes are common at funerals**: Blake E. Ashforth and Glen E. Kreiner, "'How Can You Do It?' Dirty Work and the Challenge of Constructing a Positive Identity," *Academy of Management Review* 24 (1999): 413–34.

167 **"He's not lost"**: "Tragicomedia with Comic Janice Messitte on Being a

Newly Wedded Widow," Art for Your Sake, March 20, 2014: http://art foryoursake.com/tragicomedia-with-comic-janice-messitte-on-being-a -newly-wedded-widow/.

168 **"Death ends a life"**: Robert Woodruff Anderson, *I Never Sang for My Father* (New York: Random House, 1968).

169 **when people are falling in love**: Anita L. Vangelisti and Daniel Perlman, eds., *The Cambridge Handbook of Personal Relationships* (New York: Cambridge University Press, 2006).

169 **130 newlyweds were invited**: John M. Gottman, James Coan, Sybil Carrere, and Catherine Swanson, "Predicting Marital Happiness and Stability from Newlywed Interactions," *Journal of Marriage and Family* 60 (1998): 5–22; John Gottman, *The Seven Principles for Making Marriage Work* (New York: Three Rivers Press, 2000).

170 **defines a resilient relationship**: Jane E. Dutton and Emily Heaphy, "The Power of High-Quality Connections," in *Positive Organizational Scholarship: Foundations of a New Discipline,* ed. Kim S. Cameron, Jane E. Dutton, and Robert E. Quinn (San Francisco: Berrett-Koehler, 2003).

170 **couples often find that the sparks fade**: Arthur Aron, Christina C. Norman, Elaine N. Aron, et al., "Couples' Shared Participation in Novel and Arousing Activities and Experienced Relationship Quality," *Journal of Personality and Social Psychology* 78 (2000): 273–84.

171 **In the couples whose marriages lasted**: John M. Gottman, Janice Driver, and Amber Tabares, "Repair During Marital Conflict in Newlyweds: How Couples Move from Attack-Defend to Collaboration," *Journal of Family Psychotherapy* 26 (2015): 85–108.

171 **Just three journal entries of seven minutes each**: Eli J. Finkel, Erica B. Slotter, Laura B. Luchies, et al., "A Brief Intervention to Promote Conflict Reappraisal Preserves Marital Quality over Time," *Psychological Science* 24 (2013): 1595–601.

175 **"I won't make your skin crawl"**: Allen Rucker, *The Best Seat in the House: How I Woke Up One Tuesday and Was Paralyzed for Life* (New York: Harper-Collins, 2007).

Index

ILLUSTRATION CREDITS